Coaching 101

101

Discover
the Power
of Coaching

Robert E. Logan and Sherilyn Carlton
with Tara Miller

ChurchSmart
R E S O U R C E S

St. Charles, IL 60174
1-800-253-4276

Published by ChurchSmart Resources

We are an evangelical Christian publisher committed to producing excellent products at affordable prices to help church leaders accomplish effective ministry in the areas of Church planting, Church growth, Church renewal and Leadership development.

For a free catalog of our resources call 1-800-253-4276.

Unless otherwise indicated, Scripture quotations used in this book are from the *Holy Bible, New International Version* (NIV), copyright © 1973, 1978, 1984, International Bible Society. Used by permission of Zondervan Bible Publishers.

CoachNet® is a registered service mark of Robert E. Logan.

Powerpoint® is a registered trademark of Microsoft Corp.

Cover design by: Julie Becker
Manuscript edited by: Kimberly Miller

© copyright 2003
by Robert E. Logan and Sherilyn Carlton

ISBN: 1-889638-37-4

Coaching
101

Contents

Preface 7

Acknowledgements 9

Dedication 11

Introduction 13

Chapter 1 So what is coaching anyway? 23

Chapter 2 Relate: Don't skip the small talk 31

Chapter 3 Reflect: Where are you? 43

Chapter 4 Refocus: What will you do? 61

Chapter 5 Resource: What do you need? 73

Chapter 6 Review: Let's celebrate! 85

Chapter 7 Guidelines for powerful coaching relationships 95

Chapter 8 Where do I go from here? 111

Appendix: 119
    Coaching questions
    Sample coaching agreement
    Additional resources and contact information

Preface

by Bob Logan

God-centered coaching has the power to change lives—both your life and the lives of those with whom you come into contact. Sherilyn told me about a time when she stopped at a little roadside stand to get some ice cream for the ferry ride back to Seattle. The man making the cones was friendly, and they soon found themselves talking about his double major in computer science and music and where he was headed with his career. As she was handing him the money and picking up her ice cream cone, he asked, "So what do you do?"

Sherilyn told him she was a life and leadership coach: "I help people clarify and achieve what they want to accomplish in life and work—I help them live from the core of who they are."

He smiled and said, "Oh, wow! Like you just did for me? That's cool!" Their conversation had lasted five minutes at the most. Yet in that short space of time, the ice cream man was able to get some clarity on his future, and Sherilyn walked away feeling the quiet delight that comes from being used to facilitate personal discovery.

We want to give you the paradigm and tools that you need to experience the power of coaching. You can use these tools at any time, any place, in any role. You can choose to scratch the surface, using simple coaching techniques here and there in everyday life, or you can choose to dig deep, entering into official coaching partnerships that will facilitate radical change. Either way, this book is the first step in the journey. We hope that it will be the beginning of many delightful discoveries on the ministry journey of coaching others to know and do the will of God.

I count it a privilege to coauthor this book with Sherilyn Carlton. I have long respected her insights and abilities as a coach. Many of the stories in this book stem directly from her experiences as a coach and a trainer of coaches, and her collaboration has greatly impacted and shaped the direction of *Coaching 101*. Her coaching skills and confidence are impeccable, but what I appreciate most is her tender heart toward God and her passion to help others succeed. The effective coach combines a strong spiritual foundation, relational capacity, and strategic skill—and Sherilyn embodies all three.

The ideas presented in this book are rooted in an extensive qualitative research project. Because *Coaching 101* is designed to be a basic introduction to coaching and is only the first in a whole series of soon-to-be-released resources, we are choosing not to go into depth about that research project here. In the sequel books, you'll gain more detailed research result information. For updates on when new resources will become available, please visit www.coachnet.org or E-mail the CoachNet® office at Logan@coachnet.org. You can also contact CoachNet® to get information on pursuing specialized coach training for your group or denomination.

Just one practical note: writing a book with two authors can present certain stylistic challenges. How do we identify who is speaking when? How does the reader know whose experience or thoughts are being presented at various points in the text? In the interest of clarity and flow, we decided on a simpler approach. "I" refers to Bob Logan: "When I was pastoring my first church...." Sherilyn is referenced in the third person: "Sherilyn finds that training coaches...." Everything else—the vast majority of the book—was done in collaboration. We hope that this will make your reading easier and lend additional clarity to the text.

The insights from this book come from our collective experience of over thirty years of hands-on coaching. It's our prayer that the Holy Spirit will use this experience to guide you as you embark on your own coaching journey. Our deepest hope is that God will use you to make a significant difference in the lives of others as you seek to release the potential of those around you.

Acknowledgements

Tara Miller – Wow, did your fingers do some walking! Thank you for turning tumbling words and grand ideas that we spoke over miles of telephone line into readable words.

Gary Reinecke – We appreciate your diligence partnering with Bob on the qualitative research that forms the framework for this work.

Jeannette Buller – Not only did you facilitate our work as project manager, you contributed your wisdom and encouragement.

Colin Noyes – Your insights and intuition are invaluable as always. The feedback you provided challenged us to strive for excellence.

Coaches – The stories you shared from your coaching ministries helped us understand the experiences of a broad range of coaches in the field.

Dave Wetzler – Thank you for your guidance and support throughout the journey. Thank you for enabling us to share the gift of coaching.

Kimberly Miller and Peggy Newell – Your editing and proofing work paid attention to important details in the final stages.

Julie Becker – Your graphic design of the cover and layout of the book enhances the attractiveness and readability.

God – Thank you for possibilities. Thank you for all the ways you have shaped and coached us through your Holy Spirit. We are very grateful for the opportunity to serve you and make a small contribution to the advance of your kingdom.

From Sherilyn

Mom & Dad – I have been your apprentice coach from my first breath. Thank you for making me who I am and believing that I am even more.

Renee – Your cheerleading and prayers have been a powerful force in my life. And the uncontrollable laughs that we've shared as sisters is on my list of favorite things.

Chad & Madi – Because of you, I dare to believe that the impossible is. If a picture is worth 1,000 words, I'd need 1,000 pictures to express the love, awe, appreciation, and delight for the gift God has given me in you.

From Bob

Janet – As my life partner for 26 years, I am so grateful for your love, friendship, and encouragement. Words cannot express how much you have influenced me and helped me grow personally.

Dad – Your definition of success has guided me throughout my life and ministry. Thanks for your coaching and encouragement throughout the years.

Dedication

To all those we have had the honor of coaching – You have been an inspiration and have given us the privilege of seeing God in action.

Introduction: Why coaching?

Seeing the opportunities

A year ago Joe, a recent college graduate, excitedly approached you with a proposal to start a youth group. Within a few weeks, the two of you began meeting to flesh out his ideas. *At last,* you thought, *our church's long-time goal of a senior high youth group is becoming a reality.* Joe and ten high schoolers kicked off the group with an extreme sports weekend retreat that was well received by both the kids and their parents. Just nine months later, however, you began to feel uneasy. You noticed that Joe no longer beamed every time you asked him how the group was going. In fact, as the months have gone by you have begun to sense that he resents the hours he has to spend setting up for and tearing down after each event. You wonder whether you should approach Joe but are concerned about his reaction.

After the monthly men's prayer breakfast last Saturday morning, Scott and Kevin told you about a Promise Keeper's event in your city that they recently attended. They said that experience had made them long to belong to weekly accountability groups. You smile and nod with enthusiasm even though you know there is no way you can add one more responsibility to your schedule. "Oh, by the way," the men add, "we'd love to help the church launch such groups. How can we help make that happen?"

Rebecca, a longtime church member and prayer warrior, expressed the desire to see people praying together before the services each Sunday morning. "We really need a prayer team. I wish I could help start one, but I'm not a very take charge person.

All of these situations are coaching opportunities just waiting to happen. A coach is someone who comes alongside to help others find their focus—and you can be that someone in the lives of others. You can be a coach, helping people like Joe, Scott, Kevin, and Rebecca more fully live out the calling that God has for them. A coach helps others get where they're going; they help people find their way and give them a sense of perspective. Within the framework of a coaching relationship, people can take stock of where they are, figure out where God wants them to go, and decide what steps to take to get there.

Why should I invest in coaching?

It's probably clear how coaching can help those who are being coached, but what about the coaches? Many would-be coaches are already swamped with responsibilities, feeling worn out with nothing left to give. Yet in his wisdom, God has designed coaching relationships to be mutually beneficial—sometimes they help the coach just as much as the person being coached.

Coaching can be used to develop more leaders to work with you, people who are equipped to take on more responsibility and share the load. Do you lead a ministry team? Do you work with people? Do you want to be a better parent? Are you discipling new believers? Do you want to help people establish a ministry in your church or community? The applications are limitless. No matter what your field, coaching provides solid, proven principles that can be adapted to fit your own situation.

> **Whenever you invest in developing people, your own workload decreases.**

Whenever you invest in developing people, your own workload decreases. Are you tired of being the answer-person? Start developing more people who can field the questions. Are you worn out from being the go-to person for every project? Raise up additional leaders who can oversee new initiatives. Are you shepherding too many people? Coach more shepherds to help you share the load. Are you at your evangelistic capacity? Raise up more evangelists to continue bringing in the harvest. Because you're tapping into the God-given potential of others and increasing their capacity for responsibility and leadership, coaching allows you to decrease your own workload while at the same time accomplishing more.

Take the example of parenting. As parents coach their children, the children increasingly take on more responsibility and the parents no longer need to do everything for them. Say a child is just learning to dress herself. Will it take longer for her to do it herself? Will it be less convenient? Would it be easier for the parents to do it themselves? Yes, but only in the short run. Wise parents know that in the long run it's much better to guide children toward independence. Not only will they learn to perform practical tasks for themselves, but they'll gain self-confidence. They are empowered when a parent communicates, "You can do it. I'll be here if you need help, but I don't need to step in and take over. I believe you can handle it." Moving toward independence and empowerment is an essential part of the maturing process.

Too often we forget that the role of a leader is not to do all the work alone: it's to prepare others for the work God has for them. Ephesians 4 explains that the role of church leaders is to prepare God's people for works of service, so that the body of Christ can grow and build itself up in love as each part does its work. The role of a Christian leader is to equip. And that role is not restricted to pastors and church leaders; we can all help one another prepare for kingdom work. Hebrews 10:24-25 urges believers to consider how we may spur one another on to love and good deeds. Part of our Christian responsibility is to help one another release our full potential—and much of that can be done on a peer level. Coaches are not experts or know-it-alls—they are ordinary Christians who have the opportunity and privilege of coming alongside others and helping them succeed in fulfilling their God given potential.

If calling others toward God's purpose for their lives sounds good, this book is for you. If raising up new leaders to share in the responsibilities of the ministry sounds good, this book is for you. If freeing up more of your time sounds good, this book is for you. All of these things can be accomplished through coaching. To coach someone is to make a lasting investment in the life of another person and in the kingdom of God. Imagine the impact you could have for Christ by being a Barnabas, an encourager, in the lives of others.

The Barnabas Factor

Originally named Joseph, Barnabas was one of Paul's closest companions, traveling with him on missionary journeys. Translated literally, Barnabas means "son of encouragement."

Acts 11:23-24 says this of Barnabas: "When he arrived [in Antioch] and saw the evidence of the grace of God, he was glad and encouraged them all to remain true to the Lord with all their hearts. He was a good man, full of the Holy Spirit and faith, and a great number of people were brought to the Lord" (Acts 11:23-24). That's a great description of a coach: one who is called alongside to encourage, prepare, equip, and help others succeed. Coaching is a biblical role.

Barnabas often acted as a liaison between people, building bridges to bring them together. After Paul's conversion, Paul tried to join the disciples in Jerusalem, but they were afraid of him. After all, Paul had a reputation for killing Christians. The disciples—reasonably enough—thought it was a trap. But Barnabas took Paul and brought him before the disciples, testifying to the genuineness of Paul's conversion.

Barnabas also served to bring John Mark back onto the team after John Mark had abandoned Paul and him on a previous journey. In spite of that history, Barnabas saw potential in John Mark for significant future ministry. He knew God could still use him to build up his kingdom. Imagine what that must have meant to John Mark—to have someone believe in him in spite of past failures.

Many times at seminars, conferences, or other speaking engagements, I ask people how it would feel to have a Barnabas in their lives—someone who believed in them, someone who would come alongside to listen to them, ask questions, and help them clarify where God wants them to go. I ask if they think that would be helpful. I've never once had someone tell me, "No, that wouldn't be helpful—I don't really see any need for someone like that." I never hear that. I just see a big show of hands of people who want a Barnabas in their lives. The need is there, and you can be part of the solution.

The basics of coaching aren't difficult and anyone can learn them. What does a Barnabas do? He helps people answer three questions: Where am I? Where do I want to go? How will I get there?

Where am I?

Once I got lost in a shopping mall. It was the height of the Christmas season and shopping was in full swing. Everywhere I looked I saw distractions and advertisements. Scents and sounds abounded. I knew what store I wanted to find, but amid all the crowds and confusion, I lost my sense of direction. Where was I?

At that point I did what most of us would do. I found a directory and looked for the "you are here" tab. It was gone. All I saw was a big map of the mall. Without that tab telling me where I was in the mall, the directory was useless to me. We can't take any steps toward a goal unless we first from know where we're starting. Some point of reference is needed. A good coach helps people find the "you are here" tab in their lives so they can begin taking steps that will lead them toward their goals.

Where do I want to go?

Of course, taking steps toward a goal requires identifying the destination. The problem is that toward the beginning of the journey, most people don't always know exactly where they want to go. The destination may be a bit fuzzy and even incomplete. They don't have an address and a detailed map with every street marked and labeled. Instead they begin to draw the map as they go—like an explorer. The explorer's map is drawn according to best guesses and is based on incomplete data. An explorer may have a general sense of direction and purpose, but much is left uncertain. After all, an explorer is venturing into uncharted territory and the map will need to be improved along the journey. Most people are in much the same position as an explorer: they have to draw and sharpen their maps as they go. They may have a general idea of their destination, but it's still fuzzy and without much detail.

> **Coaching is a way of improving the map as the journey continues.**

Coaching is a way of improving the map as the journey continues. It ensures that people have someone to travel alongside them as they discover their destination—someone to help them think through their options and chart their course. Christianity has never been a go-it-alone faith, in spite of our frequent attempts to make it that way. God has called us to collaborative partnerships with other believers for accomplishing what he wants us to do: "And let us consider how we may spur one another on toward love and good deeds. Let us not give up meeting together, as some are in the habit of doing, but let us encourage one another—and all the more as you see the Day approaching" (Heb. 10:24-25). God intended that believers join one another in walking down the path of growth. By walking together, we can gain a clearer sense of direction and purpose, seeing pitfalls ahead of time and discovering alternate routes when necessary. We can encourage one another when we lose sight of our destination. We don't have to go it alone.

How will I get there?

Ultimately, coaching is forward-looking and action-oriented—it provides people with the focus necessary to take their dreams and make them realities. Strategy and action steps are essential, for positive change requires a proactive approach.

God has something for each of us to accomplish. Paul wrote in Ephesians 2:10 that "we are God's workmanship, created in Christ Jesus to do good works which God prepared in advance for us to do." Jesus, when he got to the end of his life and ministry, said in John 17:4, "I have finished the work you gave me to do." Our Heavenly Father wants to create Christlikeness in our character. If we allow him to enter into us fully, he'll shape us so we can reflect him more clearly. God has given us a part to play in the advance of his kingdom. We are successful when we find out what part that is and learn to play it well. Then when we stand before God he will say, "Well done, good and faithful servant."

Coaching can help people take steps that move them toward the completion of the work God has given them to do. That's strategy—that's coaching in action. Coaches are those who recognize that they have the opportunity to participate in God's plans by coming alongside others as they seek to grow and reach their potential.

What coaching isn't

But most of us are like Moses. When an opportunity presents itself, the objections come flying. In Exodus 3 and 4, when God commanded Moses to speak to Pharaoh, opportunity wasn't the first thing on Moses' mind. Instead he responded, "Who am I, that I should go to Pharaoh and bring the Israelites out of Egypt?" A litany of other objections followed. "What if they don't believe me?" "But I'm not a good public speaker." And finally, the direct approach: "O Lord, please send someone else to do it."

When faced with the prospect of coaching, many well-meaning people assume they are unqualified. "Who, me? A coach? But I don't know all the answers. I haven't been to seminary. What if someone asks me for advice and I don't know what to say? Who am I to place myself over others?"

Questions like these reveal a misunderstanding of what coaching is and what it's designed to accomplish. Placing ourselves over others is exactly what coaching is not: it's not about telling others what to do.

Advice has little to do with it. In fact, as you read on, you'll find that giving advice is something good coaches try to avoid. Instead, they help people make discoveries for themselves.

Another question I've asked at seminars is, "How many of you know an area of your life where God wants you to grow?" Every hand goes up. We all know. Then I ask, "What do we need to make that become a reality?" No one has ever said advice. Instead I get answers like support, encouragement, and companionship. Coaching is not about giving advice—people already know what they need to work on. It's about support. They want to know they don't have to navigate the difficulties of life on their own.

Coaching is also not a matter of authority. Paul and Barnabas were coworkers; neither had authority over the other. Although we've used Barnabas as our example of a coach, he most likely learned many things from Paul as well. In some cases, a coach may be more experienced in a particular area than the person he is coaching, but not always. Many times a peer coaching relationship works best. Sometimes we just need an outside set of eyes and ears to give us a sense of perspective.

And coaching isn't about being an expert. Is there knowledge involved? Absolutely. But the most crucial knowledge focuses on areas like listening skills and asking good questions. Coaches don't need to have all the right answers so they can tell people what to do. It's not about listening to the coach—it's about helping others learn to listen to God for themselves. Can you think of a time when a friend just took the time to listen to you and helped you sort things out in your mind until you could come to your own conclusions? That was coaching.

At its core, coaching is really quite simple. You don't have to be an expert—anyone can learn to coach. In fact, you're probably already functioning as a coach in many ways. We all play the role of a coach sometimes; we just don't always recognize it as coaching. Pastor, worship team leader, parent, brother, supervisor, friend . . . we all coach someone. If you supervise people at work, you have an opportunity to be a coach. If you work on a team, you're probably involved in peer coaching relationships. If you're discipling a young believer, that's coaching too. Learning the ins and outs of coaching and some basic skills may move you into new responsibilities and new coaching relationships, or it may simply help you become a better coach where you are right now.

Coaching: an investment that lasts

As the world becomes more and more high tech, your ability to coach people—to reach out to them on a personal level—is what will separate you from the pack. Coaches make investments that last. When you work with others, you never know where they'll end up.

Dorothy once coached a young woman in her church named Lisa. Lisa was a college student at a local university, but was painfully shy and lacked confidence. Often she would call Dorothy to get input on minor decisions. Dorothy was a beginning coach, but she began noticing the trend. The next time Lisa called and asked, "What do you think I should do?" Dorothy began asking questions to draw out Lisa's own thoughts. Soon Lisa found she was able to make decisions on her own about friends, extracurricular clubs, and her major.

Over the course of the next few years, the transformation in Lisa's character was marked. She had gained the confidence to start initiating community service projects and reaching out to others. Although she was still soft-spoken and a woman of few words, her gifts in evangelism became more pronounced. In fact, she found the words she did speak had an even stronger impact because of her emphasis on quiet service. As Lisa began learning more about herself and her values, she realized that she was drawn to working with the inner city poor. Today Lisa oversees a large tutoring ministry in an underserved urban community.

The role of a coach is a significant one and we all play it to one degree or another. Yet too often it's an unexamined role. By taking the time to become aware of the ways we coach and by learning some basic coaching skills, we can make a difference in the lives of others—and in our own life. Anyone can learn coaching skills, and the dividends are great. You'll lighten your own workload as you help others develop. You'll build stronger relationships. You'll be making an investment that lasts.

That's what this book is all about—making an investment that lasts. You have the potential to do that by coming alongside others to help them succeed. As you read about coaching principles and put them into practice, you'll see how powerful coaching can be—both in the lives of those you coach and in your own life.

Through the course of this book, we'll lay out a structure and a process that can guide you step-by-step through coaching relationships. Although our coaching model is rooted in solid, qualitative research, you'll find it's written in such a way that makes it easy to put into practice. The heart of coaching is simple: you can help people significantly by listening well and asking good questions. Understanding the stages of the coaching process provides an important road map for the relationship, but each stage—at its core—is about listening and asking good questions. Those are the two most significant ways coaches help people see where they are today, where they are going, and what steps they need to take to get there.

You don't have to be an expert to be a coach. You can do it. By putting into practice the basic coaching skills outlined in this book, you can have a significant impact on the lives of others and on the work God has called you to do. We'll give you enough help to get you started, and you'll begin seeing the power of coaching unleashed in your life and ministry.

Your turn

To make reading this book a life-changing experience rather than simply something you can check off your list, we invite you to take time to reflect and practice. If you are working through this book with a team, discuss each chapter and/or do the field work together.

Who in your life has been a Barnabas, a coach, to you? What did he or she do?

To whom could you be a Barnabas? Who in your life could you coach?

Field Work: Pray and ask God to make clear to you as you read this book where you can most effectively start using these coaching principles.

CHAPTER 1

So what is coaching anyway?

What is success?

My father is an engineer and a very wise man. I asked him one time, "Dad, what's success to you?" My father replied, "I've thought about that question a long time. In fact I was about twenty years old when I realized it was an incredibly important question to ask myself. I didn't want to go all the way through life and get to the very end and realize I had missed it. So I pondered this question for several months and I finally boiled it down to one sentence: Find out what God wants you to do, and do it!"

I've never come across such a profound definition of success. And yet it's so simple. Success can look very different on different people, but its basic core is always the same: Find out what God wants you to do and do it. The role of a coach is simply to help them find out what that looks like for him or her and then help that person figure out ways to do it. Coaches walk alongside people throughout the whole process: clarifying goals, brainstorming plans, trying them out, revising them, trying again, and celebrating successes. They help people discover who God made them to be and delight in the unique mission he has called them to accomplish. Whether we're talking about a drama coach who's trying to help someone perform a part well or a swimming coach who's trying to teach the backstroke, a coach's goal is to help others succeed.

> **Find out what God wants you to do, and do it!**

The challenge of success

Find out what God wants you to do and do it. It sounds simple, doesn't it? Yet the simplicity of the definition belies the difficulty of the journey. It's hard to discover what God wants you to do and it's even harder to do it. As one leader put it: "I always thought finding God's will would be like finding a gift under a tree. Instead, I've discovered that change is difficult. I'm not going to just serendipitously arrive where I'm supposed to be. It requires effort on my part—I have to apply myself and work hard."

The journey is difficult, but anything worth doing requires effort—and in spite of the challenges, we can succeed. Understanding that success is finding out what God wants you to do and doing it can transform your life and your ministry. And coaching enables you to help others succeed also. The secret is in listening to God. If we can hear his voice and tap into the unique person he has created us to be, we will *naturally* advance his kingdom. The concept is surprisingly simple: success is listening to God . . . and responding.

Listening to God and responding

At its core, coaching is a spiritual process. Listening to God and responding doesn't always translate neatly down on paper: If you do x and y, z will result. God sometimes intervenes in surprising ways.

Very early in my ministry, we had some brand new-Christians coming into our church and I had the privilege of discipling one man just after he had come to Christ. When we disciple someone, we hope to see that person become a disciple—one who lovingly obeys Jesus' commands. It's the same with coaching. As we come alongside people to help them discover God's agenda—and cooperate with the Holy Spirit to see that agenda become a reality—they will grow in Christlike character and realize their fullest potential.

Gary, the man I was discipling, had lived a pretty rough life prior to receiving Christ. He had problems with anger, he drank too much, he smoked, he yelled at his kids, and so on. Yet he also had experienced genuine conversion and had felt the power of the Holy Spirit in his life. Where he had been prejudiced against certain groups of people before, he now felt love toward them. Gary and I were going through the normal kinds of new believer lessons and he was growing like crazy. Working with him was exciting, because I saw such amazing changes taking place in his heart.

One day Gary came to me and said, "Bob, I've got to sell my boat."

I said, "Okay."

He responded, "No Bob, you don't understand. I need to sell my boat!" He went on to explain. "I used to go out on that boat and get drunk and do all sorts of things that I'm now ashamed of. That boat is an idol to me. God showed me the verse in the Bible that says if you have faith like a mustard seed you can move a mountain. Then the Lord showed me the one about asking anything in his name and receiving it. I found more like those too! So I've been praying that God will sell my boat for me. I'm not going to advertise or anything. And I've already told God the price I want to get for it. Would you pray with me about this, Bob?"

You can imagine the dilemma I faced. Gary had called his boat an idol. In Old Testament times, you destroyed idols. You smashed them, chopped them up, and burned them. You didn't ask God to sell them for you. I also felt uncomfortable with Gary's face-value interpretation of the verses he had cited. But nevertheless, I prayed with him. I don't remember exactly what I prayed, but I do remember thinking, "Okay, God. Whatever."

A couple weeks later Gary came over. He was so excited he could hardly contain himself. "Bob, Bob, guess what? God sold my boat! I was washing my truck outside one day and this guy just stops and rolls down his window and says, 'Hey, do you want to sell your boat?'"

Now Gary was a salesman, so he was pretty cool about it. He pretended to consider the idea and asked, "Well, what do you want to give me for it?" The guy looked the boat over carefully, then named the exact dollar figure for which Gary had been asking God. He went and got the cash, gave it to Gary, signed the papers, picked up the boat, and hauled it off that day. As Gary finished telling me the story, he said, "Bob, God really answers prayer, doesn't he?"

I was blown out of the water. So many of my theological paradigms had been destroyed. I had to cancel the rest of my appointments that day to think about all of it. I went home and sat there for hours because I was so shocked. What had I just experienced? After four hours of sitting there in my favorite chair, I realized I could have discipled this guy until Jesus came back and I would have never dealt with the major issue in his life. He had so many other problems that were so much more obvious from the outside. I came to the conclusion that I am not smart enough to be the Holy Spirit. I can only draw out what is already present within a person.

The best I can do as a coach is come alongside others and help them listen to the Holy Spirit for themselves. None of us knows what God is calling others to do. Trying to push our own agenda is the quickest route to stifling a coaching relationship. Only as people discover for themselves what God wants them to do and do it will they begin realizing their full potential. As coaches, we can't play the role of the Holy Spirit. Most people know what they need to address, and we need to trust in their ability to hear the voice of the Spirit for themselves. Our job is come alongside them to draw that out, then walk along with them as they figure out what the next steps are.

Meredith's story

Meredith worked full time for an international Christian organization. Her job involved developing materials, teaching classes, organizing seminars, and attending evening training events. She sometimes traveled and almost always put in more than a forty-hour workweek. Meredith also attended seminary, where she took a demanding courseload. Although she struggled with Greek, good grades were important to her and she spent a good deal of time studying. At church, Meredith was deeply involved in leadership. She attended a cell church, where she led groups, participated in numerous outreach events, and helped with the worship team.

All the time and emotional energy Meredith was investing began taking its toll. Her health began to suffer. She wasn't getting enough sleep and felt fatigued all the time. Although she was only in her early forties, she developed heart problems. Meredith was sometimes sick for months on end, but felt like there was nothing she could change because everything she was doing was important. Her job was important. Church involvement was important. Seminary was important.

Surrounded with criticism from an early age, Meredith grew up in an oppressive and abusive environment. Consequently, she had a hard time saying no—even when she knew she was getting in over her head.

Sherilyn, Meredith's coach, began by helping her begin to explore her values. What they discovered was a life almost diametrically opposite from the one she was currently living. Meredith loved having time alone to read, space and quiet. She felt most rested when she could spend a whole day at home gardening and cooking. She longed to get married, have a family, live in the country, and grow all of her own food.

The disparity between what she wanted and how she was living was a shock to Meredith. She realized she was living on "shoulds," frantic with activity because she thought it was what other people expected of her. How could she say no to attending an outreach event because she wanted to stay home alone instead? She felt silly for even having the desire. It wasn't "important" enough. Yet Sherilyn helped her measure the cost of the way she was currently living her life and they agreed that some changes needed to be made.

Meredith began setting aside chunks of time on the weekend to spend alone, doing things that energized her. She also started saying no to additional demands on her time. She cut back on her courseload at seminary and her activities at church. Although she initially felt a great deal of fear about how others would regard her decisions, the results were exciting. For the first time in years, Meredith felt like she had time to refuel her spirit. She had the time with God that she wanted and was deepening her walk with him. The time she was still devoting to ministry became richer and more productive. Friends and coworkers commented on her renewed sense of energy and excitement.

Although Meredith initially felt confused about what she should do, at a deeper level she knew what she needed all along. She knew which activities energized her and which drained her. Yet to gain enough confidence to act on that knowledge, she needed someone to come alongside her to validate her desires and inclinations. We all need someone to stand by us and offer the grace and love of God, to encourage us to live as God made us to be, regardless of our current "performance" in ministry. That kind of love and unconditional support can make all the difference in the long-term effectiveness and joyfulness of our lives and ministries.

Lou's story

I used a coaching approach with my first administrative assistant. When Lou and I first began working together, she would check in with me frequently, "So-and-so called. What would you like me to tell him?" Instead of giving her a quick answer, I chose to engage her in conversation and help her think her way through the questions she would bring me. As we continued working together,

Lou grew more confident in leading, managing, and delegating. She was soon able to give good counsel and direction to people who called without the need for my direct involvement. Eventually she moved into the position of financial administrator. In that role, Lou gave personal oversight to a large and complex building project, which she brought in on time and under budget.

Just as voice teachers stretch the ranges of their students through vocal exercises, coaches step up the level of challenge little by little to stimulate growth. People can often do much more than they think they can, and can end up doing it very well. Many people—like Lou—may need to do something new and different and reach beyond their comfort zone to realize their full potential. Some may throw themselves into a new project, some may assume leadership of a ministry, some may return to school—the options are infinite. For others—like Meredith—reaching their full potential might actually mean doing less.

How do coaches help people succeed?

Now that we've begun exploring what a coaching relationship is and what it's supposed to accomplish, the next logical question is, "So how do we do it?"

Coaching is more an art than a science; we aren't solving algebraic equations. Instead, coaching is more like painting. Every painting will be unique, for we are all uniquely made in God's image and he has a different plan for each one of us. There are as many right answers about what God would have us do as there are people. We aren't "one size fits all"—every person needs to find out what God wants her to do personally.

Yet although it's true that coaching is more an art than a science, take comfort in the fact that coaching can be learned. The basic process is simple. In an effort to understand how coaches help people succeed, Gary Reinecke and I conducted a qualitative research project under the direction of Dr. Charles Ridley. Chuck is a professor and Director of Training in the Doctoral program in Counseling Psychology at Indiana University. He is nationally recognized in psychological assessment, multicultural counseling and therapy, organizational consultation, and ministry personnel selection. Our goal was to define the process and outcomes of coaching, creating a road map that could guide people's thinking. We conducted extensive research on an international level evaluating high, medium, and low performing coaches, and identifying the specific competencies that excellent coaches exhibit. Although we do not have the space in this book to report the results of this study comprehensively, the most foundational material we uncovered were the five Rs of the coaching process: relate, reflect, refocus, resource, review.

The Coaching Process

■ Relate — Establish coaching relationship and agenda

■ Reflect — Discover and explore key issues

■ Refocus — Determine priorities and action steps

■ Resource — Provide support and encouragement

■ Review — Evaluate, celebrate, and revise plans

This basic coaching process will be explored in much greater depth throughout the rest of the book, but the outline above can serve as a general overview. Seeing the big picture before getting into too many of the specific details often helps with clarity. By following this basic framework and practicing the coaching skills discussed later in the book, anyone can learn to coach. I've found all over the world that after I've given a brief three-hour orientation on coaching—basically what you have in this book—people can use basic coaching skills to begin helping others and be helped themselves.

Although there are five stages listed, keep in mind that coaching isn't a purely linear process. You may be well into the resource phase when you realize you need to focus on reflecting again for a while. That's okay. The coaching process is designed to be flexible. As you enter into a coaching relationship, be sure to maintain an openness to the Spirit's leading and an awareness of the natural flow of relationship.

Conclusion

Learning to become an excellent coach is an ongoing journey. If a climber is trying to scale a mountain, she may not always choose the best pass the first time. But if one route isn't working, she can always return and choose a different route to get where she wants to go. Even if we don't always do it right the first time, that's okay. Through endurance and encouragement we can accomplish our goals.

Coaching isn't just for experts and specialists. The basic methods are simple and anyone can learn them. We all need someone to spur us on toward love and good deeds, toward realizing the fullest potential that God has for us. And we all need to consider how we can help others along that path.

We need to come alongside people to help them determine the right steps, because in the final analysis, success is not measured by how many people you win to Christ, how big your church grows, how many hungry people you feed, how many missionaries you raise up, or how many churches you plant. Success in the final analysis is measured by one thing and one thing only: knowing and doing the will of God. As coaches, we have the privilege of coming alongside others to help them along their journey—to become what God wants them to become and to accomplish what he wants them to accomplish.

Your turn

How has someone helped you be conscious of the Holy Spirit's work in your life when you were making a decision? How did that feel?

Where do you sense the Holy Spirit prompting you now?

Field Work: Sit down with someone and ask him, "Where do you sense the Holy Spirit prompting you?" Spend a minimum of five to ten minutes listening. Ask no questions, make no comments, only "Uh-huh" and "Hmmm" and "Oh." When the time is up, simply say, "Thank you for sharing that with me." Journal about the experience. If you are working with a team, take turns completing this exercise. And after each person has had a chance to be heard, take one or two minutes each to tell one another how it felt to be listened to.

CHAPTER 2

The power of relating: Don't skip the small talk

Introduction

John started coaching Eric, another man at his church. As they got to know each other, John began asking Eric questions. "What energizes you? What do you care about?" As Eric talked and explored the answers to those questions, John helped him channel his energy in a focused direction. "What are your options? What do you think God is calling you to do?"

As Eric processed his thoughts, he noticed a recurring theme. Men's ministry kept coming to mind. He cared about men, their lack of community, the struggles they face trying to balance work and family commitments. Without being told what to do, Eric came away with a clear sense of direction. John's approach communicated that he cared for him deeply and was committed to coming alongside to help him accomplish what he set out to do. A connection had been made—Eric knew he wasn't in it alone.

Sometimes we can forget that at its core coaching is a relationship. It's about qualities like trust, connection, support, and understanding. The relationship is what gives power to coaching. If we skip over building a solid relational foundation in our hurry to get more accomplished, our strategy will backfire. Coaching that leaves out the relational element will be ineffective at best. Think of the people who have had the greatest impact on your life. Most likely you aren't thinking of a conference speaker or the author of a book you read. You're thinking of people who know you personally, people who took the time to invest in your life. Relationships make the strongest impact on our lives—and coaching is no exception. If you want to have impact, you need to have relationship.

Yet relationships are challenging. They don't just happen—in fact, they usually require a great deal of effort. Far from one-size-fits-all, each can be counted on to be different than the one before. Depending on the individuals involved, different relational styles and approaches will be required. To build strong, honest, effective relationships, coaches need to know themselves and those they are coaching. Building relationships will take time, but they will form the essential foundation upon which everything else is built.

Many of us assume we already know how to build relationships—and to a large extent, that may be true. However, coaching differs from friendships and other types of relationships: coaching is a relationship with a purpose. Although friendships may serve the purpose of fellowship or companionship, the purpose of a coaching relationship is more concrete and defined. When I'm at seminars, I sometimes describe the coaching relationship visually. I hold my hands parallel to each other, indicating two people in relationship, then I bring my fingertips together to indicate a common focus.

When Lana hired Sharon as a ministry assistant, they spent a morning reading about and discussing the Personal Profile System (popularly called the DiSC*), which identifies people's behavioral styles. They considered the likely ways their behavioral tendencies would interact and how that would affect their working relationship. The purpose—in this case—was getting to know each other so they could work well together. Getting to know each other doesn't always need to be this structured, but some plan should be in place. Skipping over the relationship-building phase can make others feel like projects instead of people, as if they are taking up your valuable time.

John and Eric also had a purpose. They weren't just hanging out—they were working toward a goal. John first helped Eric clarify where God wanted him to go; then they began figuring out what steps to take to get there. The eventual result was a flourishing men's ministry at their church.

Since the focus of coaching is to help the other person accomplish what God wants her to do, that person must be the one setting the

---

*The DiSC system can be obtained by contacting ChurchSmart Resources. U.S.: 1-800-253-4276. International: ++1.630.443.7926.

agenda and determining what to work on—not the coach. She comes to the coach and says, "I really want to work on this area. Would you coach me?" The two then negotiate a relationship that is defined and purposeful.

Within that relationship, the coach plays a supporting role. He may ask, "Is there any area of your life where you sense God wanting you to grow? Where do you need help developing that?" Sometimes major breakthroughs occur and the lightbulb comes on. Other times, it just provides confirmation of where the person was already going, and the coach's main task is simply encouraging the process.

So how do you build an effective coaching relationship? The two best ways to get to know others are also two of the most obvious: listen and ask questions. Yet it's surprising how often these simple acts are overlooked.

Listening as the foundation of relationships

Although there are many ingredients to a successful coaching partnership, the most important one by far is listening. It's the essential cornerstone of every relationship. How do you get to know someone? By listening. How do you build trust? By listening. How do you help people think through their goals, their options, their feelings? By listening. People want to know they are being heard. How many times have you heard yourself or others ask: "Do you know what I mean?" Real listening is rare.

> **One of the problems with listening is that it's often mistaken for doing nothing.**

One of the problems with listening is that it's often mistaken for doing nothing. Most of us have been trained to believe that someone interested and engaged in a conversation, will be talking a lot. Not talking is viewed as passive—a sign of disinterest. Yet listening and not talking are two very different things—and that distinction makes all the difference in the world to the person doing the talking.

When I was much younger, I remember being in conversation and interacting with others. I was partly listening but mostly trying to frame what I wanted to say next, so I wasn't really paying full attention to what the other person was saying. And at some level, the person talking always knew that. As I've grown in my life and my ministry, I've begun to realize the power of listening. The art of it is actually to capture what the other person is saying, and to do that without interpreting, evaluating, or guiding them in a particular direction.

Twelve-step recovery groups demonstrate the power of listening well. The group structure is simple: when one person is talking, he talks only about himself and has the floor completely until he is finished. No one jumps in and says, "Have you done this? Have you tried that? Maybe you should do such-and-such." There is no cross talk at any time during the meetings. People learn not from the advice of others, but by talking— verbally processing things aloud that they are beginning to realize about themselves. And when they are not sharing themselves, they learn by listening to the stories of others.

Listening is anything but passive. It is active and powerful, a significant tool that God has given us to use in the lives of others—for listening is the ultimate other-centered activity. A good listener focuses completely on the other person, giving that person undivided attention.

Some people are able to hear God's voice as they process with others. They may not know what the problem is—or even that there is a problem—until they start talking. A group of four women had been meeting regularly for years to talk about God and their lives. They knew one another well and each woman had seasons when it felt like not much was going on in her life. Yet they rigidly enforced their one rule: Everyone gets the floor for half an hour. Often a woman would begin by saying, "Well, not too much has been going on lately. I don't think I have much to say . . . ." And half an hour later she'd finish with "Wow, I really had a lot to say after all." And she'd walk away having heard God's voice of guidance in her life.

> **Some people are able to hear God's voice as they process with others.**

The gift of listening

Focused listening is a phenomenal gift. Imagine the feeling of having someone really listen to you for half an hour—someone who would focus completely on what you are saying, not trying to get words in, shifting the focus away from you or trying to get you to see it from another perspective.

A pastor named Dan attended a seminar on communication skills. After the lecture, all the participants were divided into groups of three.

One person was to share and the other two were to listen. Dan began sharing about some problems he was experiencing in his ministry. He received half an hour of undivided time and attention. No one interrupted him. No one gave him unsolicited advice about how to fix the problem. They just listened, nodding their heads with understanding. At the end of that half hour, Dan was almost in tears with gratitude. He couldn't remember the last time anyone had really listened to him for more than a few minutes.

I've discovered both personally and professionally how powerful listening can be. For over a year now, I've been using the following process: When people approach me after seminars and ask me questions, I respond by saying, "Tell me what you think," or "What ideas have you had?" Sometimes they bristle because they want an expert opinion, but most of the time they are quite pleased to tell me what they think and get some confirmation that they're headed in a good direction.

When I summarize what others are saying, invite them to say more, and keep unpacking their resources, they will solve their own problems 70 percent to 80 percent of the time without any input from me. In almost half of those cases, they'll shake my hand and say, "Thank you so much for your input," not realizing that I have provided no direction whatsoever.

Cardinal rules of listening

Unfortunately, listening skills do not come naturally. They need to be learned, and we all have room for improvement. The following list can serve as a guide as you work to sharpen your listening skills. As you review it, consider to what degree you already practice some of these skills. Which are areas of strength? Which are areas that need improvement? Try an experiment this week: Choose one or more real life conversations and—without telling the other person what you are doing—begin practicing the listening skills below. You'll be surprised at the results.

- **Focus:** Give undivided attention to the person who is talking, without allowing your mind to drift off toward what you'd like to say next or to concerns in your own life.

- **Summarize:** Summarizing is mirroring back what people are saying. At appropriate stopping points, reflect back what you hear the person saying, without interpreting, evaluating, or projecting feelings onto the person's statements.

- **Invite:** When a person talks a bit about a topic and then stops, ask for more. Often people will introduce an issue, then stop discussing it prematurely because they are uncertain of the interest level of their audience. We often edit ourselves as we speak because we're used to short attention spans in our listeners.

- **Unpack:** Exhaust the speaker's resources before sharing anything yourself. Train yourself to think of their ideas as more valuable than your own. For them, they will be.

- **Clarify:** Sometimes we are quick to think we understand someone, but we aren't really on the same page after all. Check your assumptions by asking, "Here's what I'm hearing you say so far . . . . Is that accurate?" You'll be surprised how often a helpful correction is made.

Take a look at the way these listening skills are used in the sample coaching conversation below:

Carl: Hi, Brian. How's your week been?

Brian: Kind of rough, actually.

Carl: Rough?

Brian: Yeah. I had a visitor show up at my group and the regular attenders didn't reach out to her much.

Carl: They didn't reach out?

Brian: No. They hardly asked her any questions. I was so frustrated with them.

Carl: Tell me more about what happened that frustrated you.

Brian: Well, they said hi at the beginning and asked where she was from, but then they just got involved in conversations with each other. The visitor just sat there looking uncomfortable.

Carl: So your group members didn't take much initiative in pulling her into the conversation.

Brian: No. I guess it's just a lot easier for them to talk to the people they already know.

Carl: Anything else?

Brian: Yeah, actually. I've been frustrated with this attitude because it's not what God would have us do, even if it is easier. Maybe I need to steer some of our group discussions toward things like outreach and inclusion even when they come at the expense of our personal comfort!

Carl: Hmmm.

Brian: You know, that's not a bad idea. I mean, there's plenty of Scripture to support that point. Maybe I could do something out of Acts next week . . . . Thanks for your input, Carl. That was really helpful.

A good coach doesn't have to say much to be effective. Carl clarified when he asked, "Rough?" He reflected back what he was hearing as Brian filled out the details of the situation. Carl then invited Brian to say more about his feelings by saying, "Tell me more about what happened that frustrated you." After listening, Carl summarized what he had heard without interpreting: "So your group members didn't take much initiative in pulling her into the conversation." It wasn't really a question; Carl just summarized and reflected it back to Brian. Ultimately, the resources and ideas unpacked were Brian's alone. Nothing Carl said was intended to steer Brian in a particular direction or lead him along a predetermined path.

Asking questions

After listening, asking good questions is the next most important skill for building a strong coaching relationship. Powerful questions can help people feel valued, which in turn will help build trust. Sherilyn remembers watching her parents interact with guests when she was a child. Her parents were active in their church and had gifts in hospitality and evangelism. When they noticed visitors at church, they often invited them home for dinner after the service. Even at seven or eight years old, Sherilyn enjoyed those dinner table conversations. The adults said such interesting things! It was only much later that Sherilyn realized that her parents' skill in asking questions had a great deal to do with how interesting those conversations were. They asked people about things they had done, things they wanted to do, and what they thought about life. They drew people out in a way that allowed them to be known.

Although there are many different ways to form a strong relationship with the person being coached, sometimes asking good questions can serve to open the door. The right questions can help establish trust and create bonds between people. Below are just a few questions that could create a doorway into someone's life. Spend some time brainstorming more that fit the context you are working within.

- What are your deepest passions? What really satisfies and fulfills you?
- What energizes you? What drains your energy?
- What legacy do you want to leave? What do you want to be remembered for?
- What are your strengths? Where are you gifted?
- What's one thing you'd like to change about yourself?

Clarifying expectations

Asking questions is also an excellent way to clarify expectations. What are you trying to accomplish in the coaching relationship? What is the other person trying to accomplish? Making sure you're on the same page at the beginning can save a lot of time and energy in the long run. After all, the job of a coach isn't to help a person in all areas of her life. Coaches aren't exalted gurus, multipurpose all-in-one mentors, able to handle anything. Establishing clarity at the outset about what you're trying to accomplish allows the coach to commit to come alongside the person to work on agreed upon areas.

Allison may come to her coach for help in creating more significant devotional times with God and deepening her prayer life. Charles may want to learn how to better communicate with his teenage daughter. Tracy may ask her coach for assistance in becoming a stronger small group leader. They all want something different out of a coaching relationship, but the key is that they decide what that is. Coaches may ask questions aimed at clarifying expectations so a point of focus can be determined, but any direction setting must be done by the people being coached—they are the only ones who can determine what areas of their lives and ministries God wants them to address.

Coming up with their own solutions

Another significant by-product of listening and asking questions, as Carl and Brian discovered in their conversation earlier in this chapter, is that people often come up with their own solutions. In that scenario, Carl made no suggestions of any kind. Brian worked out a conclusion and course of action on his own. Often if a coach listens long enough, the other person eventually says, "You know what? I think I just figured it out . . . ." Many things can be worked through without any input at all and people find they already have the answers they were seeking.

Yet for that to happen, the environment in a coaching session must be such that leaders feel valued, listened to, and respected enough to come up with their own conclusions. And in an environment like that, if you listen well and wait, people almost always do.

Stuart was having trouble adjusting to his new ministry position. He had recently accepted a staff position at a growing church that was renting space from a school. Each Sunday, he was responsible for transforming the auditorium into a sanctuary: setting up the sound system and the song lyrics on PowerPoint®, coordinating the greeters, the refreshments, and the nursery, cleaning up afterward and stowing all the gear. After a few months in the position, Stuart was feeling overwhelmed by the many tasks to coordinate, processes to develop, and pieces to fit together. The learning curve was steep, and it was all on-the-job. He was feeling the pressure.

Sherilyn, Stuart's coach, asked him one simple question: "How do you keep track of the things that you need to do or want to do?" He thought for a minute. "Well, I put them on a to-do list each day. When I have meetings with people on the teams I coordinate, I take notes in a notebook and then the paper just ends up somewhere. Sometimes I paper-clip it to my planner. I have another notebook that I keep brainstorming ideas in." He went on describing his methods for a few more minutes, then fell into silence. "I'm realizing as I'm talking that I don't have a very good system for keeping track of my work. I think that's contributing to my stress level and I need to figure out a better way to track my responsibilities. Here's what I think I'll do . . . ." Stuart had an idea about what to do without any input from Sherilyn. When coaches practice patience and good listening skills, they find people often lay out great and workable answers completely on their own.

However, instead of waiting for people to discover solutions on their own, many coaches fall prey to a common temptation: setting forth their own solutions. If someone comes to us with a problem, the default tendency for most of us is to jump in quickly and try to fix it for that person. Not only does this rob the person we are coaching of the experience of solving his own problem, but our advice often proves ineffective as well. If we have not taken the time to listen, the solutions we present will have little to no impact. Courses of action that people determine for themselves are followed with much more conviction and enthusiasm than those they are told to follow.

Remember three simple rules:

- Don't give advice.
- Don't tell people something they can discover on their own.
- Don't fix the problem for them.

Instead, give people the dignity of being able to listen to God for themselves. If Carl has a problem, asks me a question, and I give him a good answer, what's going to happen next time he has a problem? He'll come to me. But I want Carl to learn how to figure out those problems on his own. Good coaching doesn't create dependency, but independence.

Sherilyn's parents and best teachers hammered this point home over and over. When she asked, "What does narcolepsy mean?" they told her "Go look it up in the dictionary." When she was a teenager, she was helping with a summer mission project. Part of her responsibility involved lifting heavy five-gallon buckets of water and carrying them up the hill. It seemed like good weight lifting exercise, and Sherilyn got to the point where she could lift one in each hand. She wanted to know how much one bucket weighed so she asked her father, an engineer who knows these kinds of things. Instead of an answer, she was given a formula whereby she could work out the answer: one cup of water weighs this much, now you figure it out.

The vast majority of the time when people come to you with a problem, they already have the answer—or the means to discover the answer. Often when asked and given time to process, people will lay out a great and totally workable solution on their own. They simply need someone to help them draw it out and put structure to it. The impact of having someone listen, summarize and reflect back without interpretation may seem simple, but it cannot be overestimated.

Coaches don't need to know all the answers—they just need to know how to help people find them. When one coach finally grasped the simplicity of this concept, he responded with a sigh, "What a relief! How freeing not to have to play the expert. I've never felt comfortable in my coaching role before because I thought I was supposed to know all the answers and I knew I didn't. I always felt like I was faking it somehow."

Ultimately, coaching is about helping people think for themselves within the context of relationship. Solid listening skills form the heart of a good coaching relationship: they provide relational support, draw out people's best thinking, help them sort through their options, and encourage them as they make their own decisions. Through listening we form a bond with those we are coaching. And every step of the way, it lets them know that they're not in it alone.

As a developing coach, you can gain a great deal of confidence and effectiveness by honing your listening skills. Take the thirty-day challenge: Try a disciplined process of asking questions to unpack the thinking of others before contributing your own thoughts, and see how many times they can come up with solutions on their own. You'll be surprised how helpful people find the process and how many workable ideas are presented.

Your turn

When was the last time someone really listened to you? What was that like?

Field work: Try an experiment this week: be intentional about using good questions. Choose one or more real life conversations and—without telling the other person what you are doing—try asking some of the questions below and respond only with questions or comments that focus, summarize, invite, unpack, or clarify (as described earlier in this chapter). If you are working with a team, take turns listening, then give one another feedback. As a suggested discussion starter: describe a frustration you are dealing with at home or at work.

- What are your deepest passions? What really satisfies and fulfills you?
- What energizes you? What drains your energy?
- What legacy do you want to leave? What do you want to be remembered for?
- What are your strengths? Where are you gifted?
- What's one thing you'd like to change about yourself?

CHAPTER 3

The power of reflecting: Where are you?

Introduction

I went on a mountain biking trip recently. I wasn't familiar with the terrain and after a while I lost my sense of how far along I was on the trail. How much progress had I made? How much farther did I have to go? What obstacles still lay ahead? Gaining perspective is crucial when you're on a bike trip. Without that perspective, it's easy to get discouraged or sidetracked. That's even more true in life and ministry. We can get so busy with activities that we can lose focus on where we're headed and what's really important.

Gaining perspective is the central task of the reflect stage. We need a good, accurate picture of where we are, where we've been, and where we want to go. Key steps in reflecting well include celebrating progress, clarifying direction and values, and acknowledging and understanding obstacles. Reflecting well is crucial; it helps us identify our priorities and understand the reality of our situation. For so much of life, we don't really have a clear map, so getting a strong sense of perspective is especially important.

Throughout the coaching process, the more the people being coached do for themselves, the better. That's especially true of the reflect stage. The best way to help others get a clear picture of where they are and where they want to go is by drawing out their desires and then following their lead. People need to have the freedom and autonomy to set their own agenda. The questions "Where am I?" and "What am I dealing with here?" must be answered by the individuals themselves, not their coaches. When a coach says, "Here's what you need to work on," the coach ceases to be a coach and becomes an expert consultant.

Basically, the reflect stage involves becoming aware of what's going on, sorting out the various issues, deciding which ones are the most important, and committing to address them. It forms the initial launching point for the work and planning that is to come. Through listening and asking questions, coaches and those they coach can discover and explore key issues, develop a better understanding of the situation, and recognize the areas most in need of change. Remember my story of being lost in the shopping mall in the first chapter? The reflect stage is our search for the "you are here" sign. Reflection helps us figure out where we are. We need to know that before we can decide where to go.

The next section of this chapter is organized around five key coaching questions. These questions can be used to help people through the process of gaining perspective during the reflect stage.

What can we celebrate?

Sherilyn and I both begin every coaching appointment with this question or some variation on it: What good things are happening? What are you excited about? Starting out on a positive note helps people avoid the almost universal tendency to focus on problems. Our natural inclination is to look at what's wrong before we look at what's right. Celebrating the good gives us much needed encouragement and strength to face the obstacles ahead.

Obstacles, of course, are a given. Sometimes things go wrong. We were on our mountain biking trip and got winded, had to stop, maybe even took a fall and got our knees scraped . . . all the more reason for looking back at the progress made so far. The perspective gained by becoming aware of what we're accomplishing makes the pain a bit more worth it.

What's really important?

Asking people about what's really important to them helps sort out issues of priorities and values and moves them toward a sense of God's calling on their lives. We were designed to connect our work with our values, for we are God's workmanship, created in Christ Jesus to do good works. He's forming his character in us so we can accomplish the work he has set forth for us.

To do that work, we first must decide what's important, then look at the dissonance between what's important and what's thrown at us on a day-to-day basis. The plumbing starts leaking, a family crisis arises, conflict breaks out at church—situations arise that drag us off our course and pull us in different directions. Asking people what's really important helps them sort out their priorities.

One woman, when asked by her coach what was really important to her, had a ready answer: "Relationships. Investing in authentic relationships with others is what best demonstrates the love of Christ and brings people into the kingdom." Yet as soon as she said it, she realized that her hectic schedule of activities left little room for investing deeply in relationships.

Asking what's really important helps people examine their situation in light of their values and priorities: What connects you with God's call? What do you value most? What has the Holy Spirit been tapping you on the shoulder about? Answers to questions like these provide an important key for the future direction of the coaching relationship.

What obstacles are you facing?

Approaching the reflect stage from the angle of obstacles can shed needed light as well. Sometimes obstacles are legitimate: you can't commit to as many ministry opportunities as you'd like because you're in a season of taking care of elderly parents. Certain work-arounds may be found, but the basic difficulty remains. Other times the obstacles are not so legitimate—they're simply barriers we've constructed in our own minds. Either way, any perceived obstacles need to be acknowledged, for they help clarify the realities of the present situation.

This question can be asked in two different ways. The first is the way we've already addressed: What obstacles are you facing? The second takes a more internal approach: What frustrates you? Both of these are really ways of asking the same question but take into account that some people are externally motivated and some are internally motivated. If one route doesn't seem to be yielding much fruit, try the other method.

I was once coaching a pastor named Scott. When I asked him what obstacles he was facing to his goal of a more effective leadership development ministry, he couldn't come up with any. He just kept repeating, "It seems like I should be able to do this." Yet when I asked Scott what frustrated him, he found plenty to talk about. "I'm tired of the people in my congregation being so dependent on me—they check back with me every step of the way about really minor stuff. And I'm sick of constantly having to put out fires and solve problems. And I don't want to spend my whole life in meetings. My time is consumed with management problems instead of being focused on what I really want to do, which is leadership development."

As we began to unpack the obstacles Scott mentioned, he started seeing a broader picture of how those issues interacted with his values and goals. Even though he hadn't determined strategies yet, his focus was becoming clearer and he began identifying key issues to examine. Looking at obstacles can help accomplish one of the primary goals of the reflect stage: gaining a clear picture of the realities of the current situation, both positive and negative.

Yet sometimes those obstacles threaten to block our progress altogether. Sherilyn was coaching Molly, a stay-at-home mom and pastor's wife. Molly was having a self-described identity crisis, and all she could see were the obstacles. Her husband had just graduated from seminary and accepted a pastoral position, and now she was trying to figure out what that meant for her. She was having trouble sorting out her priorities within this new role as a mother and pastor's wife.

"I don't really know what to do or where I fit in," she explained. "I feel so dissatisfied with everything—my life, my mothering, my role at church—everything! My life just doesn't seem to be going anywhere. I feel awful saying this, but when's it going to be my turn? I didn't finish college, I worked my husband through seminary, and now I'm home with kids. I love my kids, but I feel trapped. I can't go back to school now because we don't have the money. In fact, we don't have the money to do anything, so I just stay home. I don't really have any friends in this community yet and it's hard coming in as the pastor's wife."

Sherilyn began to explore options with Molly. What would she like to be able to do? What would make her feel like she had a life? Molly could list possibilities: volleyball club, a mother's day out program, date nights with her husband, going to school . . . but they all cost money. Her husband had offered to watch the kids so she could have some time to herself, but she felt like she'd pay for it later. If he watched kids, he'd have to work more at other times instead of spending time with the family. Molly felt trapped, like she had no options, nothing to do, and nowhere to go. Change was impossible and she'd pay for it if she tried to do anything different.

Over the course of several months, Sherilyn and Molly worked together to clarify Molly's values. What was most important to her? To what degree was she honoring those values? What would be the results of continuing to live the way she was now? What would be the long-term payoffs of investing some time, energy and money in herself? One of Molly's top values was community, but she felt like it wasn't happening. Initially, she felt blocked by circumstances, but she eventually recognized that through her own decisions she wasn't giving community a priority place in her life.

With some prompting, Molly agreed to spend a certain amount of time and money on herself. She took the plunge and made a few changes. She started her own play group (free), joined the volleyball club, and set aside some money for baby-sitting once a week so she and her husband could have a date night. After having date nights consistently for a few months, Molly agreed that the payoff was worth the baby-sitting money. She also began to make friends through the play group and volleyball club.

Less than six months later, Molly is signed up for school part-time to finish her nursing degree. She explained, "The biggest thing for me was realizing that change was possible and that it was up to me. Most things that feel impossible really aren't."

Most people have some level of frustration about what God has called them to do. They feel they don't have the time to do it because of all the other things that sidetrack them and demand

> **Most people have some level of frustration about what God has called them to do.**

their attention. Reflecting is about shifting our focus onto what's really important, then making adjustments to our life accordingly.

Where do you want to go?

Once we've decided what's really important and then explored the obstacles, a reaffirmation of our direction is in order. At this point we need to loop back and focus on where we want to go. What's next? Given our priorities and our obstacles, what issues need to be addressed? Where do we need to focus? Although we don't need to get into the planning stage yet, we do need to shift our gaze back to the horizon and clarify our general sense of direction again.

If I am coaching someone and ask him, "What's one area where you sense God wants you to grow?" he may respond, "Quality time with God." He's addressed the first question about what's really important. We then move into dealing with obstacles, and he cites career-related demands on his time and interruptions by his family whenever he's home. After unpacking those obstacles a bit, I may then ask him, "What do you want?" (which is really just another way of asking, "Where do you want to go?").   With some thought, he shifts his focus from the difficulties he faces back to his ultimate goal and responds, "I want to create space for God in my life. I've got to figure out a way to do that." He has pinpointed his priorities and set the direction for the road ahead.

Sometimes discerning priorities can be a lengthy, difficult process; it's often challenging to draw that information out of the person you are coaching. Yet in other cases, people will begin the coaching process with very clear ideas on the areas in which they need help and in what areas they don't.

When Norm, leader of the greeter team, entered into a coaching relationship, he didn't need a lot of help with interpersonal leadership issues. His ministry was going well in that area, and he had a strong rapport with those who were serving under him. He was aware, however, of other areas where he did need help and he communicated that to his coach: "I am really disorganized. I have a hard time keeping track of logistics in my ministry. I've got scraps of paper with phone numbers on them on my desk. When I need a number, sometimes it turns up there and sometimes it doesn't. My database is just nonexistent."

Norm essentially needed help with a practical matter, and he recognized on his own that he needed to work on it. His coach said, "Okay, in this situation, here's what you can expect from me. I'll give you all the possible help I can. Let's go to work." Norm's coach explored various options to organize and helped him establish a system for tracking information that would work for him.

As a coach, it's important to follow the lead of the person with whom you are working. Keep it simple. A coach can say, "I'm here to support you. What do you need?" It's not the coach's job to determine where people need to work. If problems arise in an area they have not been focusing on, a good coach will simply ask them how they'd like to handle the situation or what they'd like to see change. If for no other reason than continued difficulties, people almost always recognize their own problem spots.

How committed are you?

Another way of asking this question is, "What are you willing to endure to see your vision become a reality?" That's the true test of our devotion. Sometimes people go through the external motions of the coaching process hoping that it will somehow change the way they feel. Yet if they haven't honestly assessed their level of willingness to change, the cost has not been counted.

Luke 14:28 says, "Suppose one of you wants to build a tower. Will he not first sit down and estimate the cost to see if he has enough money to complete it?" Change always costs—there's no way around that. The question is whether the proposed change is worth what it will cost us. For change to be successful, we need to estimate the cost and want it badly enough to pay that price.

It's easy to generate good ideas without taking action: we may say, "Yes, I'd like to get in better shape." It's even easy to try jogging once or twice. The tough part is commitment over the long haul. A lack of resolve often lies at the core of our failed attempts. And why do we lack resolve? Because we have not looked the difficulties in the face and decided, "Yes, this goal is worth the challenges I will endure in getting there."

I've always wanted to run in a marathon. I'll probably never do it though, because I'm not willing to make sacrifices in other areas of life to train adequately. I simply don't have sufficient conviction. On the other hand, I invested the time to train for extended mountain biking trips. I've gotten in shape and have enjoyed the activity. In one case I was willing to make the commitment, but in the other case it wasn't worth it to me. I'd like to run in a marathon, but I'm not willing to pay the price. There isn't enough time in life to do all the good things we want to do. We need a sense of conviction that God is calling us to a particular goal.

Dissatisfaction with the way things are is probably the single most powerful motivator for commitment to change. Only when we look around us and are genuinely dissatisfied with what we see will we commit ourselves fully to the change process. John Kotter, in *Leading Change*, writes that the number one reason why change doesn't happen is the lack of a sense of urgency. To be both hearers and doers of the Word, we must feel a sense of urgency about what God is calling us to do. That urgency flows out of a dissatisfaction with what is in light of what could be. The visualization of a better future combined with a sense of resolve can bring about powerful results.

Obtaining a commitment to address issues is probably the most overlooked task of the reflect stage of coaching. It's far too easy to assume commitment when there is none. Coaches need to ask for specifics. When will it be done? What day and time? What will you change in your schedule to free up time to do this? What will you stop doing? How realistic do you think this time line is? Asking for specifics will yield a wealth of information about a person's level of commitment. In some cases, a bit of pressing in this area will turn up strong, unspoken resistance.

> **It's far too easy to assume commitment when there is none.**

A pastor named Dan consistently had trouble keeping his working hours down to a reasonable level and committing to a day off once a week. He talked at length with Sherilyn, his coach, about how much he wanted to take one whole day each week and set it aside with no work commitments. He wanted to spend part of it with his family and take part of it alone to recharge his energy level.

Sherilyn asked him which day of the week he planned to take off. Dan hesitated. He couldn't do Mondays because of the elder meeting, Tuesdays were out because that was the only day he had time to work on his sermon . . . every day of the week was systematically ruled out. Sherilyn then asked him which of his responsibilities could be delegated to free up his time. Again, she was met with resistance. All of Dan's responsibilities were critical and had to be done by him personally.

It turned out that Dan wasn't as committed to making a lifestyle change as his previous comments had implied. If his coach had not attempted to confirm the commitment by asking which day he was going to take off, Dan would have gone on as before: talking about the importance of a day off without taking steps to move in that direction.

Role play

Let's take a look at a sample reflect conversation and unpack some more specifics about how reflection can work most effectively.

Michelle: So Carolyn, tell me about your current ministry.

Carolyn: Well, I've been trying to establish a women's ministry in the church. So far I've organized a few retreats, but not much beyond that.

Michelle: How did the retreats go?

Carolyn: Pretty well, I think.

Michelle: Tell me more about what went well. What did you like about the most recent retreat?

Carolyn: Well, I suppose the real highlight was that someone came to know Christ.

Michelle: Wonderful! I'm glad to hear it.

Carolyn: Yes, she's since gotten involved with a Bible study and has really been growing.

Michelle: That's great. What were some other strong points of the retreat?

Carolyn: We had some really dedicated volunteers to plan and coordinate the weekend—they did a great job with all the details. And the activities were wonderful. Some of the women told me afterward that the pacing of the weekend and the activities offered really gave them a chance to get connected with other women in the church.

Michelle: That says a lot. Enlisting volunteers and creating real times of connection can be some of the most difficult things to pull off.

Carolyn: Hmm. I guess so. I hadn't thought of it that way before.

Michelle: How were you thinking of it before?

Carolyn: I guess I was just focusing on the things that had gone wrong.

Michelle: Such as?

Carolyn: The overall turnout was pretty low—only about 20 percent of the regular attendees went.

Michelle: Hmm. Any idea about what could have caused that?

Carolyn: I suspect now that we didn't advertise it enough. We put an announcement in the bulletin, but I think a lot of people didn't read it. We should have found some creative ways to advertise it from up front.

Michelle: That sounds valid. Anything else that gave you concern?

Carolyn: Well, the speakers were okay, but the topics didn't seem terribly relevant.

Michelle: How so?

Carolyn: The speakers seemed to assume that the women who attended were mostly married, stay-at-home moms when we actually had a pretty high percentage of career women and singles. I think they felt a little left out.

Michelle: Yes, knowing your audience is certainly important. (Pause) Taking a step back and looking at the overall women's ministry in our church, what do you see as the most critical areas to focus on right now?

Carolyn: I see the need for more ongoing ministry instead of just retreats now and then. I'd also like to see us delve more into community outreach. I'm not sure what all of that looks like though. As a new leader, I feel like this ministry as a whole just lacks vision and direction.

Michelle: Of all the things you just mentioned, which ones seem the most important?

Carolyn: I think vision and direction. I can't really get the other areas together until I have a clear direction to lead people and a vision to inspire them.

Michelle: Is that then the area you'd most like to see us address together in the future?

Carolyn: Yes, that would probably be the best place to start. I'll brainstorm some ideas on that area before our next meeting.

The reflection phase is a time for getting specific about the past and the present. During their coaching conversation, Michelle and Carolyn spent a while exploring what had gone well and what had not before they moved on to sorting, prioritizing, and committing to issues.

Notice that Michelle started by celebrating progress. She asked Carolyn how the retreat went and continued unpacking her comments. When Carolyn gave brief, vague answers such as "Pretty well, I think," Michelle asked for more: "Tell me more about what went well. What did you like about the most recent retreat?" That question served to highlight positive areas. Sometimes our minds race ahead of us toward all the things that haven't been done or that haven't been done well. Carolyn acknowledged that she had been focusing on the negatives; her coach's questions drew out the positives.

The biggest temptation during the reflect phase is to jump forward to next steps before taking adequate time to evaluate what has already taken place. At the beginning of this conversation, Carolyn said, "So far I've organized a few retreats, but not much beyond that." Thankfully, Michelle resisted the temptation to speed forward to asking, "So what should we do next?" Instead, she spent some time processing what had taken place up until then with the women's retreats. She wanted to address the question, "What ground have we covered so far?"

Carolyn then did think through some of the negatives—obstacles that had bogged down the retreat—and sought to learn from them and use the information strategically in the future. Yet after examining some of the problems, Michelle helped Carolyn shift her attention again to the overall ministry and asked her what she believed were the most critical areas to focus on. After Carolyn had generated several ideas, Michelle helped her decide which were the most important, then ended by obtaining a commitment to address the agreed upon priority issues.

The power of questions

It has probably become clear by now that asking good questions is an absolutely essential part of the coaching process. Every stage of the coaching relationship should be laced with powerful questions. However, since the reflect stage begins the exploring of significant issues, this seems like an appropriate place to explore further the art of asking good questions.

Powerful questions make a big difference. They can unlock doors that the best statements cannot penetrate. One of the cardinal rules of creative writing is, "Show, don't tell." Likewise, one of the cardinal rules of coaching is, "Ask, don't tell." Never tell people something they can discover on their own. Think back on your teachers in college or high school. Who taught you the most? The teacher who read his notes aloud while you dutifully copied down information? Or the one who managed to launch a spirited, relevant discussion in which the students did most of the talking and arrived at their own conclusions? Good teachers, like good coaches, ask instead of tell. They push, challenge, and even play devil's advocate to make sure you've thought through your position thoroughly.

One coach remembers a history professor who made his subject matter come alive by the way he used questions: "What would you have done if you were that king?" "How do you think they managed to overcome that problem?" "What's going to happen when inflation skyrockets like that?" The students began considering history from a personal perspective—and suddenly it made much more sense and seemed far more relevant and interesting. Asking good questions is vastly more effective than merely dispensing information.

So what makes a question good? Good questions don't have to be complicated to be powerful—simple queries like "So what's next?" can produce a wealth of insight and change. In fact, one simple rule of thumb will carry you far: ask open-ended questions.

An open-ended question is one that cannot be answered with yes or no. If you ask people, "What issues do you see as the most critical right now?" they must think independently and generate options. On the other hand, if you ask, "Don't you think meeting our budget is the most critical issue right now?" they can only answer yes or no—and based on the way the question was phrased, they might easily assume the right answer is yes.

Most of the questions we ask are closed. A closed question is one that doesn't open up more territory for discussion or seek to uncover new information. When we ask closed questions, we are often trying to limit other's options or guide them toward a predetermined conclusion. Think of a trial lawyer's cross-examination: "Did you or did you not pick up the knife?" The yes/no response that is called for eliminates any chance for explanation of circumstances—the question was designed to trap. On the other hand, the defense attorney may ask the same question in a different way, an open-ended way designed to allow the witness to be heard: "Tell us, in your own words, what happened when you walked into the room."

Parents are notorious for asking closed questions: "Did you hear me?" "Do you want to be grounded again?" "Did you break that?" These aren't really questions at all. No response is called for, as the answer is known to all. They are rhetorical flourishes—just another way of making statements. Questions should never be used as a more subtle method of telling somebody what to do.

Of course, not all bad questions are as obvious as the examples above. Many times we fall unconsciously into a pattern of asking closed questions. We ask, "Do you want to address this issue next week?" instead of "What would you like to address next week?" We're all guilty of it sometimes. The only solution is awareness and practice. We need to catch ourselves asking yes/no questions and think of ways to rephrase them as open-ended questions.

Remember that coaches ask questions for the purpose of helping others discover what God wants them to do. Use people's own stories and experiences to draw out feelings, desires, and goals. Let's say someone had a bad experience at church. She had wanted to help out with the hospitality team before and after the service, but instead had a conflict with the person leading that ministry. Her coach could ask, "What would you have liked to have been different?" or "How could you approach the situation differently?"

Avoid the expert syndrome

An added benefit of asking good questions is decreased pressure on the coach. One of the biggest reasons people avoid stepping into a leadership role like coaching is the fear of not having all the answers. A coach doesn't need to have all the answers, only some good questions. For most coaches, that's a big relief.

When Sarah, the leader of a small group, realized her group was growing too large to be effective, she approached Lou as a potential leader. Lou's immediate response was, "But I don't know enough to lead a group. What if they ask me doctrinal questions that I can't answer?" Sarah reassured her that expertise was not required. "Being a leader doesn't mean you have to know everything. I'm willing to serve as your coach, so when you get stuck we can work it through together. Besides, the technical kinds of questions you're concerned about generally don't get asked anyway. It's the real life stuff that gets asked. And when you don't know the answer to those questions, ask the group what they think. Leading a successful group isn't so much about answering questions as it is about asking them."

As with any kind of ministry, the most important qualifications for coaching aren't about what you know—they're about who you are. You don't need to know everything. When you run into a roadblock, ask the person you're coaching: "Where do you think we should we go from here?"

In fact, it's an advantage not to have all the answers. Asking powerful questions is like holding up a mirror: it simply shows what's there. A mirror doesn't tell a person what he should see—or what the coach sees—it just provides a way for a person to make personal observations and discoveries. Not having answers provided frees people to think for themselves. Good questions encourage creative thought and allow people to reach their own conclusions.

Remember to use silence as a tool. One of the most common mistakes of new coaches, new teachers, and new group leaders is not waiting long enough for responses after a question has been asked. Don't fear silence; it gives people the necessary time to process their thoughts. Always wait at least five seconds. Count if you have to—it can feel much longer than it is.

In some cases, you'll encounter resistance when you refuse to play the expert. Stan was designing a website to enhance the ministry of a group of overseas missionaries. His plan was to use it for both communication and fund-raising. He structured the site, almost like a mini-business. Visitors had the option to purchase souvenirs from the region where the missionaries were serving and a portion of the proceeds went to support their ministry.

Stan regularly asked his coach specific questions regarding the website—financial and business advice, technical concerns, editing help, feedback on public relations approaches, ideas on how to raise more money. Often Stan's coach responded with other questions or comments designed to provoke thought: "What do you think would be best?" "What would you like to see happen?" "Tell me about your options." Stan grew increasingly frustrated. He wanted someone to give him answers to his questions. He and his coach had had a fundamental miscommunication: Stan didn't want a coach—he wanted an expert consultant. Good coaches resist being the answer person; they recognize that their primary role is to be the question person.

Sensitivity to the Spirit

Becoming aware of ways we can ask powerful questions can help all of us learn to be better coaches. Skill training is helpful. Yet all the training in the world cannot replace sensitivity to the Spirit of God. Sometimes he prompts us to take unusual directions and surprises us with his presence. Listen to one of Sherilyn's experiences:

She was coaching John in his career. He felt unhappy with his current job and kind of lost. He wasn't sure if it was the job itself or if he needed to change careers altogether, but he just had this general sense of heaviness and loss. Although he was already very well educated and had earned two master's degrees, he just didn't feel satisfied and questioned whether he was in the right field.

He'd asked Sherilyn to focus on his career. He was not involved in ministry and had no connection with church, but during one session she had this flash that she needed to ask him about God. It made her nervous because she didn't know him well and didn't want to ruin their relationship, but the sense that she needed to do this was strong. So Sherilyn said to him, "This may seem like a strange question, but where does God fit into all of this?" He paused and then started talking about how God was only for holidays because the only time he went to church was Christmas and Easter. He believed in God, sure, but he wasn't part of John's everyday life.

What came out of that question was a discipling relationship in which they focused on making God a part of every piece of John's life. He started having daily devotions and was able to slow down the pace of his life. Before he had been the kind of person who literally could not just talk on the phone; he had to talk on the phone and weed the garden. But now John started sitting still to read his Bible and pray. Friends noticed the difference in him. At the end of their coaching relationship, he said, "I had no idea we were gonna go here. If you would have told me that we'd end up talking about God I would have thought you were crazy. But I think God knew what I needed—it wasn't a new job or career move. I needed a spiritual focus. What I needed was God. I feel like a light has come on and I didn't even know it was dark." And it all came about because the Holy Spirit kept insisting that Sherilyn ask him that question. Although it was difficult at the time, she's so glad she listened.

Conclusion

The reflect stage serves to give people a picture of where they are and how far they've come. Only once they've gained that perspective are they positioned to make informed choices about directions for the future. The coach's role is to guide people through the process of exploring key issues, developing a better understanding of the current situation, and recognizing areas most in need of change.

During this critical stage, questions are one of the coach's most powerful tools. In fact, questions are the only effective way to help people reflect on where they are and what issues need to be addressed. Be sure to take a look at the exercises listed in the "Your turn"—investing time refining these important coaching skills will yield powerful dividends.

Your turn

Field work: Some people find it helpful to frame questions in terms of information, awareness, and action. Thinking in these categories can help coaches construct questions that dig deeper. Consider the following situation: someone tells you she is not satisfied at work and is thinking of changing careers or exploring other vocational options. Brainstorm some open-ended questions you could use from each of the categories below.

Information:

What are you looking for in a career?

- _____

- _____

- _____

- _____

Increase awareness:

How might a career move impact your family relationships?

- _____

- _____

- _____

- _____

Promote action:

What are some possible first steps you might take as you explore your options?

- _____

- _____

- _____

- _____

CHAPTER 4

The power of refocusing: What will you do?

Introduction

A couple of years ago I went to see the eye doctor for a routine checkup. He said, "Bob, the good news is your eyes are in great condition. But I should let you know that in a few years you're probably going to need reading glasses." Reading glasses: that hit me hard. Only old people need reading glasses. I just sat there in silence for a minute. I must have looked stunned because the doctor said to me, "Don't worry, Bob. It's just a normal part of the aging process." That wasn't exactly comforting. I went home and mulled it over.

After dealing with my own mortality issues, it struck me that my diagnosis had a parallel in the area of leadership. I realized that all effective leaders have bifocal vision. You have to have long-range vision to see where God wants you to go in the future and you have to have short-range vision to see the individual steps it'll take to get there. If you have only your destination in view as you walk, you become so focused on the horizon you could fall into a hole. On the other hand, if you walk with your eyes down on each step you take, you can get completely lost. You need to keep your eyes on both, shifting back and forth periodically. Creating that healthy balance is the goal of the refocus stage.

Essentially, refocusing constitutes the planning stage. After gaining a general sense of direction in the reflect stage, we can now move on to giving our vision some definition and specificity. It's time to create a game plan and come up with concrete steps that can take us where we want to go. If someone decided during the reflect stage that he wanted to do a better job of fathering, now is the time to figure out what that's going to look like. For one dad, it might be getting more consistent with discipline. For another it might mean taking his kids to the park more often. For either father to make progress, a plan must be made. That would mean deciding what better fathering would look like for him, then figuring out what to do to make that vision become a reality.

Refocusing acts as the bridge between good intentions and actually realizing those intentions. We all have dreams and desires, but we need to get them translated into specific action points if we hope to see them become a reality. Refocusing confirms our destination, direction, and priorities, but it also translates them into concrete steps that will help us move forward. To refocus well, we need to keep shifting our eyes back and forth between the horizon and the individual steps along the way.

Doing the work required during the refocus stage can make a significant impact; it can bring about desired results and help avoid anticipated pitfalls. Charles was reworking the organizational structure of his church. Through coaching with Sherilyn, he'd already figured out where he was—stuck. He had realized that the current structure was capping growth—the leadership wouldn't be able to handle any further expansion and no one was training new leaders. He wanted to structure ministry teams in such a way as to plan for the next hundred rather than just take care of the people they already had. The church was currently caught in a cycle that precluded further growth, and Charles wanted to break that cycle. The next step in his process was to ask, "So what exactly do I want to accomplish and how can I get it done?"

Sherilyn helped Charles experiment with various brainstorming strategies. He wrote questions for himself as launching points. He created lists of important tasks and prioritized his pastoring schedule to focus on ways to make progress rather than just maintain. He made more lists of tasks that could be delegated or discontinued altogether. Sitting at his desk with a notebook in front of him, he drew graphs, giving shape and structure to his ideas. If person X coaches three people . . . . and slowly a chart was formed.

Even in the absence of immediate results, Sherilyn could see Charles' excitement growing. A positive shift in his outlook was becoming apparent: "Hey, this could work. I have a sense of direction. This is something bigger and better than I had before. I can see the potential here." By thinking through some of the possibilities in a more concrete way, he found himself looking at a big picture that could continue to get bigger. Suddenly the vision seemed attainable. Charles was completing the work of the refocusing stage: gaining a sense of forward movement, figuring out more specifically where God wanted him to go from here, and strategizing ways to get there.

Barriers to successful refocusing

Many attitudes and misconceptions conspire to keep us from finding out what God wants us to do and doing it. As you look over some of the more common obstacles discussed below, consider which ones block you most often.

False beliefs about planning

One barrier to the planning process is the belief that to plan is to constrict. To set goals might hamstring some other unseen potential, so it's best to keep our options open so we don't miss any opportunities that might arise. One coach described the dilemma this way, "There's a real resistance to the idea of putting anything down on paper because people assume they won't be able to change it. I try to communicate that plans are meant to be flexible. They're not written in stone. They're not the Ten Commandments. If a plan's not working, you can evaluate and make adjustments—or even throw it out completely. That sometimes helps alleviate people's fears that if they set goals they can't change them. The options are still all before them. It's just a matter of choosing which one they want to pursue."

Planning actually provides and promotes freedom. We budget our time and money in order to have more, not less. A financial budget allows us to spend our money on what we really want instead of whatever comes to mind first. Without that budget, if something truly important comes up at the end of the month we're likely to be already out of money. Planning is the same way—it gives us the freedom to choose what we want instead of being at the mercy of circumstance.

Others think of planning as unspiritual. To be guided by the Spirit, this theory goes, one must be unstructured and spontaneous. If you think of it in advance, it must not be of God. Yet God himself has a plan in the flow of history. He laid out his design before the beginning of time. Created in his image, we are also planners. As Jesus taught in Luke 14:28—"Suppose one of you wants to build a tower. Will He not first sit down and estimate the cost to see if He has enough money to complete it?" To be godly, we are to be guided by the Spirit as we make our decisions, keeping enough flexibility to adapt our plans according to his leading as we go. A godly worship leader has a plan going into the service but also a spirit sensitive enough to what God might be doing to make modifications as he goes. God can lead before and during—to be led by the Spirit means both.

Fear of failure

The potential for failure is the unspoken reason many of us resist planning. We think, "If I set goals and then don't meet them, I'm a failure. But if I don't write anything down, then whatever happens is okay." Yet that approach doesn't give us any sense of progress. Where do we want to be in a month? In six months? In one year? Without a plan, we usually don't wind up anywhere at all. Clarifying our vision and planning on the front end provides a sense of purpose and commitment. It can make the difference between getting somewhere and never trying. If we allow fear of failure to stop our efforts before we begin, we'll end our lives wondering what we could have done.

Living by "shoulds"

Often people go about trying to achieve their goals the way they think they should instead of the way that would work best for them. It's as if someone who wants to get in shape but has never exercised before says, "Starting tomorrow I will exercise every day for an hour." That's probably not the best approach for a person who's just starting out. Setting the standard too high at the beginning because we think that's what we should be doing is an almost certain setup for failure. Smaller, more manageable goals at the beginning will probably prove a much more successful route in the long run.

We need to be careful not to allow ourselves to be boxed in by the way others do things. We don't have to get up at the crack of dawn to have devotions because that's the right way to do it or the spiritual way to do it. Afternoons or evenings may work better. Coaches need to be aware of the times when people are making themselves miserable under the weight of false expectations and give them the permission and encouragement to change. Each person needs to explore the ways that will work best for them, instead of struggling along with the way they think should work. The result will be a realistic action plan that is personalized to fit an individual's schedule, lifestyle, and personality.

Sometimes we even choose the wrong goals—the ones others think we should have instead of the ones we really want. Encourage those you are coaching to examine their chosen goals and the reasons they chose them. When people select goals they don't truly desire, they seldom succeed. Remember that there's a big difference between refocusing and simply trying harder at something that's already not working. Trying harder is rarely the answer—usually it's either the method or the goal that needs to be changed. The most powerful and compelling visions are those we develop on our own, not those we allow others to choose for us.

Negative self-talk

We all have them—those little voices in our head that say: "You aren't smart enough to do that." "What will they think of you if you fail?" "That's a stupid idea." "You're not good enough." "You're going to let people down." "They'll be so disappointed in you." "You'll never stick with it."

It's time to hear those voices for what they really are: spiritual strongholds that Satan uses to persuade us to think badly of ourselves and to prevent us from doing what God would have us do. The fear induced by negative self-talk is one of Satan's most powerful weapons. Jane, who wanted to start a women's ministry in her church, explained her hesitation in terms of negative self-talk: "Whenever I think about taking steps in that direction, I hear this voice in my head saying, 'No one likes you. They're not going to follow your leadership. Even if you do manage to get started, no one's going to come. This is never going to work.' So I just avoid the antici-pated rejection and failure by not trying."

Strongholds like these keep us from taking the risk to step out and make positive changes. Coaches would do well to encourage periodic evaluations by asking, "What attitudes cost you the most in terms of satisfaction and happiness?" Whether it's the inability to forgive, constant worries about what others are thinking, or replaying past failures, those answers will help identify Satan's strongholds and strip away their power.

What do you want to accomplish?

The first refocusing question asks us to confirm or clarify our goals in light of the present realities. We have now moved from the general desires of the reflect stage, "Where do you want to go?" to the more specific goals of the refocus stage, "What do you want to accomplish?" Good goals are concrete and measurable: I want to develop a strategy for recruiting leaders for my ministry; I need to figure out how to get greater participation from the people in my small group; I want to plan the launching of this new ministry; I want to take definite steps to improve my spiritual growth. The more clearly you can define the end, the more successful you will be at figuring out a strategy to get there.

During the process of goal clarification, the coach's task is to keep unpacking people's ideas. Continue asking questions that force them to look at the end result and clarify what they're trying to accomplish. "You said you wanted to exercise more; what would being fit look like for you?" Listen, summarize what you're hearing, then ask for more, "What else?" In doing so, you're helping them see the contrast between where they are right now and where they would like to be in the future. They are articulating, defining, and clarifying what needs to change.

Many people find it helpful to think three, six, and twelve months into the future. Once they have a clear grasp on where they want to be, they can work backwards to figure out what steps it will take to get there. Sometimes people will brainstorm a lot of goals, more than they can feasibly accomplish in the near future. To help them narrow it down, you might ask, "If you could only have one goal, one thing you want to accomplish in the next three months, what would it be?" Narrowing down goals helps people set priorities, deciding which are the most important or the most strategic. Sometimes they realize that their goals act as stepping-stones to one another. Accomplishing one will help them accomplish a second, related goal.

> **If you could only have one goal, one thing you want to accomplish in the next three months, what would it be?**

What are possible ways to get there?

Once people establish their goal, they often make the mistake of coming up with only one way to accomplish the goal, then run down that path without looking back. To make better decisions, they need to first multiply the number of options available. The more options generated, the better the final decision is going to be.

If your goal is to get across a stream, what options might be available to you? You could jump. You could pole vault. You could build a catapult and sling yourself across. You could wade. You could hop across on rocks. You could saw down a tree and walk across. You could walk down the stream until you find a bridge. There are a lot of ways to cross that stream. Some options may not be as workable as others: catapulting might be fun in the air, but what about the landing? Some may require additional resources: is a saw available? Yet the time for evaluation is later. For now, the task is simply to free up creativity and generate as many options as possible. Sometimes unworkable solutions will lead to workable ones if you let your mind wander down that path. The best solutions usually come near the end of the brainstorming process, not the beginning.

As a coach, keep pressing for more possibilities. Summarize what they've said so far, then ask, "What else?" When you get to the point where you've unpacked all of their ideas, you might want to throw in a few of your own. Sometimes people get stuck. Your input may lead them to generate some additional options. Remember that you need to have at least three viable alternatives to make a good decision. If you only have one truly workable option, you don't really have a choice. And to get three viable options, you'll probably need to generate at least ten possibilities.

Continued pressing for additional possibilities may cause more action-oriented people to freeze. Others may get stuck during the brainstorming stage because they believe they have to think their way down the whole path. In those cases a coach might ask what some possible action steps might be that could help them accomplish their goal.

Let's say you're working with a ministry leader who wants to develop a gifts mobilization system. You ask, "What options do you have?" and she gets stuck. Her mind is too far ahead, focusing on what actions can be taken and how all the pieces fit together. You might then take a step back and try asking, "If people were getting mobilized according to their gifts, what are some things you might do to help that happen?" "Well, the pastor could teach on it, ministry consultants could interview people, small groups could discuss it, we could do it through the newcomers' class, we could offer an inventory and a seminar . . . ."

Thinking about actions—individual steps and pieces—instead of options helps some people brainstorm more effectively. Actions can readily be translated into options later. Often the best solution is a combination of action steps. The ministry leader may ultimately decide to offer a seminar on gifts followed by ministry appointments for all existing church members, then offer it on an ongoing basis as part of the newcomers' class. In order to arrive at this conclusion, multiple ideas had to be generated.

Which path will you choose?

We've arrived at the point of decision: it's time to commit to a particular strategy and path to accomplish the goal. After generating a range of possibilities, we can move ahead into evaluation and selection. Having good options is essential for making wise decisions, for we need to choose a plan that fits the individual situation.

Let's look again at the example of selecting a gifts mobilization system. If the person you're coaching is in a church where the level of reading skills is low, she'd probably want to work with oral strategies rather than written ones. Maybe she could conduct giftedness interviews instead of offering a written test. Find the most appropriate option for the people you're working with: consider adaptability, affordability, time constraints, and overall fit.

A common temptation is to take a solution that worked for someone else and import it wholesale into a different situation. In most cases, it just won't fit. A full-blown gifts mobilization system that worked well for a megachurch may not work at all in a small church where a more personal approach would be better. It's like David wearing Saul's armor: the armor itself may be perfectly good, but David isn't comfortable in it and can't move around. It's not a good fit. We must think creatively to find solutions that work well in the given situation.

Bill, a very social leader, may throw great parties and use them as a way to reach people and draw them into his group. That same strategy, good as it may be, may not work for Jane. After taking her own personality and inclinations into account, she may recognize that she's more effective in one-on-one ministry and will fare better by connecting with people privately. Don't look at what works for others; consider what will work for you or for the person you're coaching.

A good action plan needs to be realistic and functional. We need to take current life circumstances into account and recognize that we are not always going to be at our optimal level of functioning. Darryl had had a busy six months. Within that time period, he'd been in a car accident, had medical work done on his teeth and jaw, been in physical therapy, missed time at work, moved his office to a new location, and lost his mother. Now his son was getting married and Darryl was trying to settle his mother's estate, sell her house, take care of legal and medical issues regarding the car accident, and catch up at work.

He was overwhelmed. His coach, Sherilyn, listened as Darryl expressed his frustration: "Plus I'm supposed to keep up with the rest of life too—all the ordinary things. When am I supposed to pay my bills and mow my lawn? I'm ordinarily a really competent person, very organized and efficient. Now I'm behind at work and can't seem to get myself unburied. I know how to do all this stuff I'm dealing with. I feel like I should be getting it done and feel guilty that I'm not."

Sherilyn emphasized all the traumatic changes that had recently taken place: "You've experienced multiple losses and to expect usual functioning isn't realistic. You aren't being weak or incapable; you're being human. It's okay that this is hard. Do what you can and that's enough." Darryl broke into tears. Those words freed him from the tyranny of his own expectations. After that, he and Sherilyn worked on setting realistic goals, finding strategies for organizing his tasks and breaking them down into manageable pieces.

Life is a process, not a conclusion. We never arrive. As we grow, our goals will change with us and we'll need to continue refocusing throughout our lives. As we do so, we need to

Life is a process, not a conclusion.

be sure to set goals that are consistent with who we are and where we are. Our goals and action plans need to be brought in line with the desires of our hearts and with how God made us. Differences in people will be reflected in differences in decisions. Evaluate your life holistically, recognizing that what you do must flow out of who you are. Being and doing are inextricably linked.

What will you do?

"What will you do?" asks us to develop a specific action plan. We need to look at the who, what, where, when, and how. What action steps need to be taken? Who will take them? When will they be completed? How will they be accomplished? Be sure to remind the person being coached that she doesn't have to do it alone. In many cases, she can team together with others.

The most important thing here is to be specific. The major reason people don't accomplish their goals is because they just have general intentions, but the vision has not been translated into concrete action steps. A small group leader may want to multiply his group. Yet if no date is set and no new leaders are contacted, the chances of spontaneous multiplication are small.

One of the best questions a coach can ask at this point in the refocusing process is, "What do you sense God wants you to do between now and next time we get together?" Every little piece of the plan doesn't have to be figured out, only the next step. After the person takes that step, he can sit down with his coach, celebrate progress, then figure out the step after that. A complete, polished plan isn't necessary; what's necessary is the process of moving forward and refining the plan as you go. A climber may want to get to the top of a mountain. She has chosen a path, but after she begins she realizes she must get across the stream. Once she's across, she finds she must scale a rocky ledge. She still has the same goal in mind, but since she hasn't been down this path before, she doesn't know every step of the way beforehand. She'll have to improvise as she goes.

Refocusing is a dynamic, ongoing process of planning. The plan itself is nothing. Planning as a process is everything. The plans we develop are a snapshot of our best guess as to how we should proceed. Once we begin, we must keep changing our plans to fit with reality or they become irrelevant.

How will you measure your progress?

When people are on a journey, they need road signs along the way to let them know they're making progress. As they pass through cities and regions, the destination feels more and more within reach. Likewise, when we move toward our goals, we need some milestones along the way to let us know how we're doing. The small successes and accomplishments let us know we're moving ahead.

Consider how the accomplishment of a goal can be broken down into parts. Let's say a person is trying to lose weight. The ultimate goal might be twenty pounds, but that number may seem far out of reach, especially at the beginning. The person may even feel discouraged to see that much work ahead and lose motivation. Yet if the goal is broken down into five-pound increments, losing those first five pounds may mark a kind of celebration.

For every major goal of the person you're coaching, brainstorm together to see what some key milestone markers might be, then set up times to check in to see what kind of progress is being made. If a leader has a six-month goal of building a particular team, ask what specific things he hopes to accomplish. The first milestone might be to recruit team members, the second might be to train them, and the third might be to develop a plan of action with the team.

In most cases, it's helpful to check progress periodically but not to monitor too closely. The person who wants to lose twenty pounds may not want to weigh themselves every day—once a week might be better. Progress may be irregular, but regularly scheduled check-in times and milestone markers provide a sense of progress and accountability.

Another way to look at measuring progress is to ask the person you're coaching, "If you were to evaluate whether you're being effective, what would you measure? What evidence would you look for?" A small group leader may want to see the group members reach out, lead people to Christ, and assimilate them into the group. The leader and her coach may come up with several possible ways to measure effectiveness. Have all members of the group identified specific people they want to reach? Do they pray for those people at least once a week? Do they have regular contact with them? Have they invited them to visit the group? This approach breaks down the process, so people can measure whether they're doing the right kinds of things to help them move forward.

A cell group leader who wants to develop an apprentice leader may have in mind a list of specific tasks the apprentice will need to master. He may need to learn how to open with an icebreaker, lead worship time, facilitate a discussion, and prepare a lesson. Each time the apprentice reaches one of these milestones, he has the opportunity to celebrate and ask what's next. Breaking bigger goals into more manageable pieces can help people maintain a sense of progress as they work.

Conclusion

Deep, lasting change doesn't just happen—it requires planning and strategizing. As coaches, we need to help people pinpoint their areas of blockage, then guide them as they come up with concrete steps that will move them toward their goals. Encourage bifocal vision in those you coach. People need both the long-range vision to see where God wants them to go, and the short-range vision to see the individual steps it'll take to get them there.

Doing the hard work of the refocus stage is often what makes the crucial difference; it can bring about desired results and help avoid anticipated pitfalls. The bottom line of the refocus stage is asking people what the next step is, for analysis alone can't get them where they want to go—action must follow.

Your turn

What do you see as the major challenges/temptations of the refocus stage for the person being coached? What about for the coach?

Field Work: Find someone willing to help you practice your coaching skills—a friend, a spouse, or someone on your team. Ask that person to tell you about a significant project or goal she is working on and practice the tasks of the refocus stage. At the end, ask her for her reflections on the experience.

CHAPTER 5

The power of resourcing: What do you need?

Introduction

Back in college a good friend of mine and I went backpacking. I had never been backpacking before—I was a novice. Don, on the other hand, was an experienced outdoorsman. He'd been an Eagle Scout and came prepared with a backpack full of gear. We hiked for hours then arrived at the first campsite only to find that there was no water. I couldn't believe it. We were miles away from anything, night was fast approaching, and there was no water. How were we going to camp here?

I may have been worried, but Don got excited. He produced water-purifying pills from his backpack and started digging for water. Discouraged and thirsty, I wandered off to survey the area. Just over the next hill I discovered a faucet. When I turned the handle, water gushed out. I then did what any good college friend would do: I came back and watched Don dig for another ten minutes or so. Finally, I made a casual suggestion: "It might be a little easier to walk over that hill and use the faucet."

Sometimes people just need to get a little better connected with the options that are available to them. A coach's role is to connect those they coach with the needed resources and help them look beyond their immediate circles for possibilities. Resourcing often means the difference between struggling to make something work alone or getting better connected to make the road easier.

How do we as coaches determine if and when someone needs resources? In most cases, people will just ask for them. However, they may not be quite so direct as saying, "I need some resources," so coaches need to be listening carefully. If someone says, "Well, our action plan sounds good . . . but how will I do it?" a good coach will recognize it as a possible request for resources. Many times people will set a goal, come up with some action steps, and then get stuck on making those action steps work. Having the right resources on hand may be just the prompting they to keep moving forward.

At the end of one coaching relationship, Sherilyn asked a pastor she'd been working with what made the most difference in him being able to accomplish his goals. Originally he'd been frustrated with facilitating his leadership community meetings—he felt lost in terms of specific ideas about what to do and where to go. He told her how much he appreciated the resources she suggested: "Just walking through all the material available on the CoachNet® website gave me hope that there was something I could do about my frustration."

Using resources effectively is more than just an add-on; it can make the difference between people reaching their goals or not reaching them. One pastor wanted to implement coaching in his church and had tried for a while, but it just wasn't working. Those who were designated as coaches didn't understand what they were supposed to be doing. They met with leaders over lunch, asked how they were doing, and then just talked. The leaders didn't find it particularly helpful and everyone involved wondered why these extra meetings were necessary at all.

About that time, the pastor attended a coaching seminar and learned about the five Rs: relate, reflect, refocus, resource, and review. He went back to his church armed with material to train his coaches. Now they had purpose, structure, strategies, and a process to follow. They were then able to work together to make coaching effective in their church. Finding the right resources can make all the difference.

What resources will you need to accomplish your goals?

Once the person being coached has clarified his goals during the refocus stage, the next question to ask is, "What resources do you need to get there?" Resourcing means applying the right tool at the right time. A competent surgeon not only knows how to use each of his instruments, but also knows in what order to use them and what purpose each one is intended to accomplish. To perform a successful operation, the surgeon needs to be able to see the big picture and understand how all the pieces fit together.

If someone is running a seminar, she'll need to have various resources lined up to make it happen: a reserved location, presenters, refreshments, registration cards, possibly some advertising . . . the list goes on. The more pieces of the puzzle that are anticipated in advance, the better. As new needs become apparent, modifications will need to be made.

It's one thing to have a plan but another to have the resources to implement that plan. Resourcing means more than than just recommending a good book. Consider the full range of diverse resources—these may include time, money, connections, knowledge, experience, personnel, support, training opportunities, curricula, music, websites, PowerPoint® presentations, and forums for discussion and feedback. Some imaginative brainstorming can help people avoid being boxed into using only one or two of the many avenues available.

Sarah had already determined that her goal was to have God present in all aspects of her life, and had decided on the action steps of a daily devotional time and a monthly spiritual retreat. But what would she do during those times? Sarah felt stuck. She had never been able to stay consistent in her devotional times before. When she would sit down for time with God, she'd realize ten minutes into it that her mind had wandered. Then guilt would prevent her from trying again the next day. The thought of a daylong spiritual retreat was daunting: "If I have that much trouble staying focused during a fifteen minute devotional time, what on earth will I do for a whole day?" Sarah had a course of action but needed resources that would help her stay the course.

Together, she and her coach, Sherilyn, brainstormed a list of activities she might do during devotional times or retreats. They tried to find a variety of options that might work well with Sarah's personality and interests instead of trying to force more structured methods that didn't fit her.

Sarah felt more confident as she packed for her spiritual retreat. She pulled down a couple of favorite worship CDs and picked up a devotional book at the store that she'd been wanting to read for a long time. She threw her sketch pad and pencils into her backpack, knowing that drawing brings her into a mental state of relaxation and openness. She brought her running shoes, for she planned to jog through a neighborhood that she knew needed spiritual renewal and pray for the people living there. As Sarah zipped up her pack, she felt set up for success rather than afraid of failure.

What resources do you already have?

Sarah already had access to many of the resources she needed. She already owned CDs, a CD player, a sketch pad, pencils, and running shoes. Others were readily available: she bought a devotional book she'd been wanting to read. Once a person has decided what resources are necessary, the next step is taking stock of what she already has and what's easily obtained.

Consider resources that are available before deciding to develop new ones. Someone who is facilitating a women's Bible study may want to look through some existing study guides before beginning to write her own. Christian leaders often spend enormous amounts of time working on a project when many quality resources already exist that can save time, money, and energy. One important task of coaching is guiding people in the direction of existing, readily attainable resources that can be useful to them given where they are right now.

A few men at a smaller church were meeting together to plan the launch of a men's ministry. As the group brainstormed, one member realized that a lot of the questions they were asking had already been answered on a men's ministry website he had visited recently. He told the team leader about it and that leader found a lot of useful information there about how to recruit men to ministry and how to develop male leaders. The referral to that resource saved hours of work for the team. Most people have more resources at their disposal than they think; it's just a matter of finding the right places to look.

What resources are missing?

After gathering existing resources, some gaps are bound to remain. Effie approached me one Sunday after a newcomers' class at the church where I was pastoring. She was a young woman in her early twenties, married with two children, and our church was quite small at the time. She told me how much she had enjoyed the class and how she had discovered her spiritual gifts of leadership and mercy. Effie then began telling me what types of compassion ministries our church needed to provide outlets for those gifts: "We need a ministry to bring food to people when they are sick or have new babies or when there's a death in the family." I thought for a few minutes and said, "Effie, you're absolutely right. And you're now in charge of seeing that all that happens."

The first thing Effie did was start praying. She soon began to recognize the resource shortages she was facing. A ministry of the scope she envisioned would require a good deal of coordination and communication. She was a visionary leader, but she would need an organizer if she was going to pull this off. She recruited Judy, a woman in the church with the gift of administration, and Judy created a system for organizing and rotating volunteers and for communicating needs when they arose. Together, they launched a ministry called the Care Team.

Effie soon realized she would need at least ten volunteers to avoid the same few people always making meals and burning out. As she recruited people in the church to join the Care Team, she passed their names on to Judy, who plugged them into the system. However, as Effie talked to potential volunteers, she saw that buying the extra groceries would be a stretch for some. Others wanted to serve but felt that their cooking skills were insufficient. Both money and culinary skills were resources necessary to the success of this ministry. By pairing people together, she was able to spread the load and fill in those resource gaps. Some people even made it into a social occasion, shopping together, then holding impromptu cooking lessons.

Soon the parents of new babies had meals provided for two weeks. Permission was obtained to set up buffets in people's homes after funeral services. Non-Christians came to faith in Christ, attracted by how well the body of believers cared for one another in times of need. As the church grew, the meals ministry eventually involved over two hundred people and ran on a budget of less than $200 per year. By identifying and providing missing resources such as an administrator, volunteers, and money, Effie built a successful, growing, and life-transforming ministry.

Where will you find the resources you need?

Finding resources can often be challenging. We live in the information age: books, seminars, tapes, and websites abound. Yet that very abundance can get in the way of finding what's needed. With so much out there, where do you start? Many coaches aren't particularly good at suggesting the perfect resource. Instead, think networking. Who's well connected in a particular area? You may not know the answer yourself, but you probably know someone who does. With a few strategic calls, people can usually access the information needed.

One resource elusive to most of us is time. Time constraints can be best addressed by first looking at what shouldn't be filling up our days. Consultant Peter Drucker writes, "I have yet to meet an executive, regardless of station or rank, who could not consign 25 percent of the demands on their time to the wastebasket without anyone noticing their disappearance." That's a strong statement—of the thousands of leaders Drucker has worked with, he hasn't found one who isn't wasting 25 percent of his time. Adding more and more tasks to our already busy schedules isn't the solution. Instead, we need to learn how to trim and prune. God provides all the time necessary to do what we need to do, but if we squander portions of that time, we may find ourselves with too little left over.

A commonly overlooked resource is other people.

A commonly overlooked resource is other people. Often we feel we have to meet our goals on our own. Instead, we need to recognize that God has placed others in our lives for a reason. We can build teams, drawing on other people's gifts and mobilizing them to do what they are motivated to do. Delegating tasks not only frees up our own time but empowers others.

If experience is needed, consider who has it and how you can learn from them. A new, inexperienced youth director might be able to visit a church with a well established youth ministry and observe. If money is needed, brainstorm possible places to get it. Or consider where the existing budget can be trimmed to free up the necessary money.

A coach's role is to find ways to help people think through creative options for finding what they need. In some cases, people can locate ministries or churches that aren't using certain items. Hope International Bible Fellowship is a lower income church in an inner-city area. One of their ministries involves providing training in computer skills to help people secure employment. Hope always has a need for computers, so they seek out organizations and individuals who are updating their equipment and ask for their old systems. For their purposes, older computers are fine. They just need basic word processing; it doesn't have to be the most up-to-date technology. Creativity and adaptability can play a critical role in finding the needed resources.

What can I do to support you?

Coaches are often uncertain how involved to get during the resourcing stage. Should they give suggestions? Should they let the person being coached take the lead? What would be most helpful? The best way to find the answer is to ask the person being coached, "What can I do to support you?" Sometimes what's needed most is a simple introduction or connection. Sometimes a referral to written material would be welcomed. Sometimes help is needed in removing an obstacle to resources. Often prayer and encouragement are the most essential factors.

Coaches are sometimes hesitant to ask because they fear they won't be able to deliver. What if someone asks for Sunday school curriculum options when the coach has no knowledge in that area? No coach, no matter how skilled, is going to have all the answers. That's okay—like those they're coaching, coaches were never intended to go it alone.

Resourcing is all about making connections. The coach may not know much about Sunday school curriculum choices, but she may know an experienced Sunday school teacher. Coaches don't have to know everything; it's much better to know who knows, then work within the body of Christ to make connections. A good rule of thumb is: If you don't know, know where to go—the reference librarian and the bookstore manager are your friends.

If you don't hit on the right resource the first time, you can always try again later. Opportunities will continue to present themselves. Resourcing is an ongoing process, not a one-time event. Learn to know when to go back and revisit the resourcing stage. The resource stage is probably the area where the coach needs to be most flexible.

Although a good coach can help by being willing to network and connect, he needs to be careful to avoid overproviding. When a coach falls into the trap of feeling responsible for tracking down and researching all the necessary resources, he robs the person being coached of valuable experience. Just as children grow to be more self-reliant when their parents allow them to struggle a bit and work to earn privileges, those being coached grow stronger through the experience of following up leads and searching out the necessary resources.

Real-life resourcing

Let's take a look at a conversation that demonstrates what resourcing can look like.

Annaleise attended a church in the inner-city, where the needs of the surrounding community are great. She had a particular burden for the adolescent girls in the neighborhood. Many became pregnant at an early age, dropping out of school and becoming single parents or entering into abusive relationships. Annaleise had a vision for launching a crisis pregnancy center out of the church to help these girls. After talking over her idea with one of the pastors, Annaleise began working with a coach. Reggie established a trusting, supportive relationship with Annaleise and walked alongside her as she reflected and refocused, sharpening her vision and creating a plan of action.

As they approached the resource stage, Reggie asked Annaleise what resources she thought she might need to accomplish her goal. As they brainstormed, Annaleise's list grew longer and longer, and Reggie jotted down the major points as she talked.

"Well, I definitely can't do this alone, so one of the first things I'll need is a team."

"What types of people might you need on that team?" asked Reggie.

"I'll definitely need people who share my vision. But more specifically, I'll need some lay counselors. And then I'll need some people to train those counselors. The counselors will need to be trained in listening skills, abstinence counseling, evangelism, and maybe some cross-cultural issues."

"Yes, you would need trainers knowledgable in those areas," agreed Reggie. "Who else might be helpful to have on the team?"

"Well," considered Annaleise, "with the high Hispanic population in our area, it would be nice to have some people who are bilingual."

"Good point," Reggie said, nodding. "Anyone else?"

"Hmmm. Not that I can think of right now. But I'll probably come up with more as I go."

"Yes, sometimes that's the way it works. Other than your team, what are some additional resources you think you might need?" asked Reggie.

"We'll need to set up an office. Then we'll need supplies: pregnancy tests, pamphlets to take home. We'll also need a referral system, since we may need to refer our clients to adoption agencies, medical clinics for the uninsured, alternative high schools. We'll also need to do some type of advertising or community awareness campaign so people in the neighborhood know these services are available. Why have a crisis pregnancy center if no one knows about it?"

"Good. What else?"

"Well, I'd also like to find some way of assimilating the girls into the church. But that could be another whole ministry, and I don't really have any ideas about how to do it," said Annaleise.

"Remember you don't have to do this all alone," said Reggie. "That's why you have a team."

"Yes, maybe I could recruit someone with skills in evangelism and assimilation who could find a way to plug people into the church." Annaleise jotted down a few names.

Then Annaleise sighed and put her head in her hands. "There's so much! I'd also like to start a crisis phone line, put on an abstinence seminar . . . . I know those things will probably have to wait until later, but even now I'm realizing that I'm going to need a whole lot of resources to even get the basic services of the pregnancy center up and running. How on earth am I going to find all of that?"

"I know it can feel overwhelming at first," said Reggie, "so let's back up a little bit. Let's take a look at what resources you've already got." He handed her his notepad listing all the resources she had mentioned.

"Wow, this sure is a long list," said Annaleise as she scanned down it. Her eyes stopped on one line. "Well, I do already have the office space lined up. Pastor Dan said I could use the back wing of the church building. It's a good location with an entrance that is more private and less visible from the street. Some of the girls might have felt strange walking into the front of a church building and past all the staff offices, so this is much better. And we've got plenty of room in that back wing."

Annaleise continued looking down the list. "I guess that's the only resource I've got completely lined up . . . . Oh, and Donna told me she would make up some pamphlets for the girls to take home. She's a graphic designer. I just need to let her know what content we want to include."

"So you've got office space and pamphlets. How are you set for team members?" asked Reggie.

Annaleise considered. "Although I haven't officially lined anyone up yet, I don't think I'll have much difficulty getting some lay counselors. I've already talked with several people who are interested. Some of them are bilingual too. Plus Pastor Dan said I could make an announcement in the service to recruit more volunteers."

"Great. Sounds like you're off to a good start with volunteers. Some resources you already have—like the office—and others are readily available—like the lay counselors and the pamphlets." Anything else on your resource list that's readily available?"

"No, I think that's about it."

"Okay, so what's missing?"

Annaleise looked down her list. "That leaves trainers, pregnancy tests, advertising, a church assimilation strategy, and a referral network."

"Did you mention earlier that you had someone in mind who might be a good person to find ways to assimilate people into the church?"

"Oh yeah. Lisa. I'll ask her to pray about it. She is so gifted in evangelism—she'd be great at finding ways to plug people into the church."

"Yes, that might be a good area to delegate. As you said, it could be another whole ministry. It's good to try not to take too much onto yourself," said Reggie. "So that leaves trainers, pregnancy tests, advertising, and a referral network. Where do you think you might be able to find those resources?"

"Well, I suppose I could ask local businesses about advertising. Some might be willing to sponsor the pregnancy center or display ads or pamphlets in their women's rooms," said Annaleise.

"Good idea. What else?"

"I'd like to get a radio spot, but we'd need to do some fund-raising. We'll need to do some fund-raising for the pregnancy tests too. I guess I can look into that."

"Remember you don't have to do this all yourself, Annaleise. You're building a team."

"You're right. I'm starting to feel overwhelmed," she said.

"How can I help you?"

"Well, I have no idea where to start on getting trainers and a referral network. I just don't know people with that kind of skill or knowledge.

I don't know how to train lay counselors; I don't know about local adoption agencies or schools. I'm just not sure where to even begin."

"I don't know about those kinds of issues either, but I do know someone you might want to talk to. She's been a nurse for fifteen years and has gotten pretty well connected in the health field—I know she's familiar with adoption agencies and abstinence programs. Talking with her might be a good starting point as you build a network of people in the field."

"Thanks. I'll definitely get in touch with her," said Annaleise.

"Great. Let's touch base again in a couple of weeks and see where you are at that point. Maybe we'll have some more leads to follow up."

Conclusion

Gathering and using resources well is more than just an add-on—it can make the difference between a good idea and a bona fide reality. Annaleise will never be able to make that pregnancy center a reality through planning alone, no matter how clear her vision. Resourcing is where her plans will really be put to the test.

For most people, resourcing goes hand in hand with the implementation of the action plan. A constant interplay exists between executing the individual steps of the plan and finding the the resources required to carry out those steps. Taking the time to gather the necessary resources is like filling in mortar between the bricks of the action plan; it holds the whole structure together and allows the bricks to function as they were intended.

Your turn

Think of coaching relationships you are currently involved in or expect to be involved in in the near future. What resources might be necessary?

What relational networks are you aware of that could help you point people to additional resources?

Field work: Start a list of good resources. To get started and see a sample of the resources that are out there, you might want to visit two coaching-related websites—*www.coachnet.org* (Christian) and *www.coachville.com* (secular)—and consider the benefits of subscribing.

Chapter 6

The power of reviewing: Let's celebrate!

Introduction

After God created the world, he surveyed his work and saw that it was good. He took the time to sit back, observe, and consider—he wasn't immediately off to the next project. As people created in his image, we are designed to operate the same way. Our tasks may not be as big as God's, but it's good and natural for us to evaluate our accomplishments and celebrate the work we've done before moving on to what's ahead.

The final stage of the coaching process is the review stage. At this point, we look back over our progress and ask, "What has been accomplished?" and "How far have we come?" Although we're often tempted to skip this phase and move on to the next project, the growth potential of the review stage is considerable. It provides the accountability and encouragement to stay on track. It's about celebrating the past and looking toward the future. Reviewing successes builds the strength and courage to take another step of faith. Never underestimate the power of taking the time to look back over past accomplishments and celebrate them. That process brings about the maturity that comes with honest self-evaluation, gives us much needed encouragement for the road ahead, and provides a sense of satisfaction over a job well done.

After leading his people through the wilderness for forty years, Moses climbed Mount Nebo to look out over the Promised Land. God showed him the whole land as far as the western sea. That was his gift to Moses—he allowed Moses to see the end product of all his labors and to know that the Lord's promises were not in vain.

Reviewing can often change our perspective entirely. Jeff was working with Sherilyn to create balance between his spiritual life, family, and ministry. As a pastor, he felt burdened by constant demands on his time, and his spiritual and family life were suffering. The question he was asking himself was, "What takes priority and how do I live accordingly?" He created separate goals for each of these three areas of his life and was trying to keep them in balance.

When he and Sherilyn got together for their monthly meeting, she asked, "What successes have you had?"

Jeff shook his head. "This past month hasn't been good at all. I'm really falling behind on my ministry goals and action steps." He went on to describe sick kids, missed meetings, and family issues that were taking up his time. He and Sherilyn began dialoguing. At the end of the coaching appointment, Jeff stopped. "Actually," he said, "I just realized this was a great month. This month I lived according to my values and priorities. I made choices that put my family ahead of my work, which is what I've been trying to do all along. When I look at the big picture, this was a really successful month."

Although Jeff started his coaching meeting feeling discouraged, he ended it with confidence and enthusiasm. Realizing that he was getting closer to living according to his values renewed his commitment to move ahead. He and his coach recognized that as a big victory to celebrate.

What's working?

This first question is essentially a call to celebration. Sherilyn and I both use some form of this question to begin every coaching session. Most people tend to get too focused on the problems and on what's not working. Instead, we encourage them to start by reminding themselves of what is working. Very often, our plans and goals are not all-or-nothing propositions. Some areas are working and some are not. We aren't all success or all failure. Starting with an eye toward the positive helps us gain momentum and realize that we are making progress.

Elizabeth had accomplished considerable goals through coaching. One evening she and her coach Marie celebrated by going out for coffee. As they sat outside, Elizabeth told Marie, "Your encouragement is at least half the reason I was able to do this." What exactly was it that made such a difference to Elizabeth?

As they worked together, Marie had continually refocused Elizabeth's attention on her accomplishments. The encouragement Elizabeth drew from that perspective motivated her to move forward. She found that focusing on the positive boosted her resolve in a way that fear of failure and criticism never had.

Sherilyn makes a practice of starting every coaching conversation by asking, "What wins have you had since we last talked?" and concluding each session by asking, "What was your 'ah-ha' from our conversation today?" She spends time each session celebrating wins and reviewing what has been learned. The resulting perspective often provides those she's coaching with the encouragement to keep going.

Asking about the "ah-ha" moments—those times when the light bulb suddenly goes on and a discovery is made—can be surprisingly powerful. When Sherilyn asked a pastor named Andrew what his "ah-ha" was, he responded, "As I've talked I realized my self-worth is associated with my ministry position instead of with God's definition of success. I think I need a paradigm shift: For whom am I working—God or the church? Is my success rooted in others or in God?" After that realization, Andrew began working fewer hours but accomplishing more. He used to spend a great deal of time trying to keep everyone happy, which left him exhausted and dissatisfied with his level of productivity. Now he has redirected his focus toward the long-range goals he feels God has called him to accomplish and feels more successful than he ever did before.

Sometimes we can forget our successes when we are faced with problems or are busy focusing on our failures. Built-in celebration time is a good way to remind ourselves of what we've already accomplished and reinforce our priorities. At the beginning of each coaching relationship, Sherilyn asks every person she coaches to list their top ten values in order of priority. She then has them rate each value on a scale of 1 to 10 according to how well they feel they are honoring those values in their lives. After three months of coaching, she asks them to rate their values again and see how the scores have gone up. Many people don't realize how many positive changes they've made in just a few months until they see their scores side by side.

Everyone needs to stop and take time to notice what's working.

Everyone needs to stop and take time to notice what's working, even if the overall goal has not yet been accomplished. Maybe the relationships on a team are working well. Maybe the preparation is being done faithfully and well. Positive changes are cause for celebration.

So what does celebration look like? There are as many ways as there are people. Usually verbal affirmation or acknowledgement from a coach goes a long way. Sometimes more tangible rewards are in order.

Sherilyn describes her experience with celebration: "At times I've sent an e-card or a note in the mail saying, 'I know this has been hard for you, but congratulations! You've been wanting to do this for a long time.' I've also encouraged some people to give themselves a reward. They decide ahead of time what their reward will be. Some people have chosen a day at an amusement park; some have chosen to take time off to sit and read a book; others have gone to get a facial or manicure. Most of the time after a big milestone has been reached, I suggest postponing our next appointment. I tell people, "You've worked hard. It's time for a break. Take the time you would have spent meeting with me and go do something fun—take a bubble bath, go on a hike, go to a bookstore." The key is to actively look for what's working and find ways to celebrate it.

What didn't work?

After asking what worked, we also need to ask what didn't work. Together, those two questions serve to assess progress. Only once we see the reality of the situation can we make improvements. So before proposing any changes, take the time to pinpoint specific areas that, for whatever reason, aren't measuring up to expectations.

Maybe a leader in charge of newcomer assimilation wants to know why new people at church aren't making connections. Something seems to be blocking that process. Upon further probing it becomes apparent that church members are greeting the newcomers initially, but not doing any follow up. In this case, finding out what's not working leads directly to an area that needs improvement.

In other cases, our expectations are set too high. The perception of success doesn't take the reality of the situation into account. A church planter who has reached three or four families in a couple of months had expected to reach fifty. An evangelist brought several new people to Christ but had envisioned reaching a hundred. Are their efforts truly not working or have they just set their initial goals at an unrealistic level? Asking about what didn't work can open up whole new areas for thought and discussion.

Sometimes follow-up questions are necessary to help people determine what's not working. Consider some of the following possibilities: How is your stress level in this area? Where do you feel stuck? In what areas do you feel like you are trying to fit a square peg into a round hole? What are you feeling guilty or discouraged about? If you had a Magic Effectiveness Wand, over which of your efforts would you wave it? Fill in the blank: "I've been trying and trying to _____ but it's just not working."

Assessing areas that haven't met expectations makes sense, at least on paper. Yet coaches often encounter resistance. In many cases, a fear of failure prevents people from looking back: "What if I assess my progress and it's not all good?" People fear that past failures will rise up to shame them. Instead of learning from past mistakes, they reason that what's done is done and there's nothing they can do about it now anyway, when actually the opposite is true. Past failures provide a wealth of useful insight . . . which leads us to our next question.

What are you learning?

Whether plans are going well or poorly, there are lessons to be learned. Without taking the time during the review stage to ponder and consider them, those lessons can slip by unnoticed. Too often we are all action—and action without reflection generally amounts to a great deal of wasted energy. Without considering what God is teaching us through our experience, we're bound to repeat mistakes. We also run the risk of not repeating the good, productive actions we've taken.

As a coach, if you walk people through the process of thinking about their actions, you'll increase the probability that they'll be more effective in the future. If left to their own devices, most people don't slow down enough to do this on their own. The pace of life is hectic, and most of us would rather act than reflect. We harbor the belief that just sitting there thinking isn't doing anything productive. Yet thinking well requires a tremendous amount of mental energy and focus. Jesus regularly set aside time alone to think, pray, and meditate on the will of the Father. He also provided time for his disciples to rest and process what they had experienced.

As a coach, encourage people to reflect on what they are learning through their experiences. Ask follow-up questions: What else? Tell me more. Summarize their responses. Practice reflective listening to mine the wealth of their experience, remembering that God grants us wisdom as we learn through our successes and our failures.

I was recently coaching a leader who was trying to develop an evangelistic ministry. It had been experiencing some growth but had been a bit of a struggle. When I asked him what he was learning through his experience, he thought for a moment and said, "What we've been learning is to focus on what we're good at. We've discovered that what really works for us is when our people connect with other people. We need to create opportunities where people can have those kinds of relationships. What we need to do is focus on what we're good at." Taking the time to think about what he learned helped this leader gain focus and learn from the past.

What needs to change?

The very nature of plans is that they can be changed—the best plans are designed with built-in reevaluation times. Given an initial set of circumstances, we can make reasonable assumptions about what it will take to reach our goal. Yet once we begin taking steps, something unforeseen will almost certainly happen. Making midcourse corrections and alterations to the plan at that point is not only necessary, but good. Any competent sailor knows how to make adjustments to the course when the wind changes. Sometimes arising through error, sometimes through unexpected success, changes of some kind are bound to occur.

Cheryl's Bible study group was popular and had grown quite large. Yet she approached her coach and told him that she felt burned out and didn't want to lead it anymore. Sean recognized that Cheryl was under a good deal of personal stress and encouraged her in her decision to take some time off from leading. Yet they were both concerned about making the transition a redemptive one for the group.

When Cheryl told the group about her decision to take some time off, they were disappointed. "What are we going to do?" they asked. "We all really want to continue doing this." Two members, Doug and Chris, described how influential the Bible study group had been in their lives and how much they wanted it to continue. They concluded by asking Cheryl for a new leader. She smiled and said, "Well, I don't have any spare leaders I can take off the shelf and plug in, but I would like to ask the two of you to pray about leading it yourselves. I've seen leadership gifts in both of you and would be willing to coach you if you decide to lead."

By the following week Doug and Chris both decided that God was calling them to take responsibility for the group. They recognized it was too large to lead effectively, so they divided it and each facilitated one group. Both Bible studies are still going strong and Doug and Chris have turned out to be effective, gifted leaders.

Cheryl commented on the situation afterward. "It was as if my need for some time off opened the doors of opportunity for new leadership. There was no sense of strong-arming Doug and Chris into anything. It was more like I was simply providing the encouragement for them to do what they already wanted to do."

Ultimately, midcourse corrections allow us to learn from past mistakes and offer the chance to capitalize on current opportunities. It has been said that the man who does not learn from history is doomed to repeat it. Midcourse corrections are the way to break out of that cycle. Likewise, if you hold too tightly to your original plan, you may miss options and possibilities that present themselves.

What else needs to be done?

Those seasons when midcourse corrections require us to reevaluate our strategy often create openings for new action plans and projects. Upon closer inspection, change almost always presents us with fresh opportunities. Completion of a previous project—whether successful or unsuccessful—frees up time to channel in a new or related direction.

Mark started on staff at a church six months ago as the new children's programming director. There was no previous children's church director and the volunteer-run child care system was in disarray. He looked to his coach for support during the challenging transition he saw before him. Initially, quite a few adjustments needed to be made. Yet after Mark created a new infrastructure for the existing children's church program, his coach helped him begin looking for new opportunities. Now that Sunday mornings were running more smoothly, he found he was able to launch some outreach programs geared toward parents in the neighborhood. The vacation Bible school week brought in a large number of kids from the community and their parents started asking questions. When they visited the church, the children's programs were ready for them.

Even changes we perceive as negative often hold the seeds of new opportunities. The refreshment team at another church was completely falling apart. Offerings were down and the church was on a spending freeze. Volunteers were increasingly sparse and the same few people seemed to be taking care of refreshments every week. After a couple of announcements brought no response, the staff decided a redirection of resources was in order. They channeled the money that had been going for refreshments toward a church planting effort that was just beginning. The existing volunteers, freed from their previous responsibilities, were encouraged to get involved in other ministries in line with their giftedness. One began teaching the sixth grade Sunday school class and another started a missions team. Both money and time were redirected into ministries that were proving themselves more productive.

Remember that any ideas about new action plans or projects must come from those who are being coached. Good coaches won't start giving suggestions or assignments at this point; they'll ask questions designed to provoke thought and bring about the person's own God-given vision for the future.

Perhaps one of the most overlooked benefits of asking what else needs to be done is that it helps prevent stagnation. If we have a system or lifestyle in place that we never question or evaluate, it can grow ineffective without our even realizing it. We are tempted to sit back and say, "I have arrived." Be careful not to confuse that attitude with celebration. When we celebrate, we validate our legitimate sense of accomplishment but are also spurred on toward growth. Especially in the area of ministry, we must keep changing and growing or die out. Asking what else needs to be done can help avoid that attitude of "I have arrived" and the stagnation that goes along with it.

Paul and Jean were strong visionary leaders. They had some wonderful proposals for community outreach, and their coach, Craig, helped them build some infrastructure and put their ideas into action. At that point, Craig suggested evaluating the ministry, doing some fine tuning, and looking at what else needed to be done. They exchanged glances and said, "Thanks for all you've done to help get things off the ground initially, but we've got a lot of ministry experience. I don't think we need your help in this." Craig bowed out. Sometimes when leaders resist reviewing and evaluating, the best thing to do is to let them go. After all, as coaches we can make suggestions, but ultimately the decisions need to belong to those we are coaching.

Things didn't go as planned. The ministry never completely took off. It sputtered, got started, then stalled out, and eventually went by the wayside. Through that process Paul and Jean learned more about themselves and eventually recognized that even the most experienced leaders can use an outside perspective or another set of eyes.

Craig wisely decided to forgo the "I told you so" speech but chose instead to make himself available when they were ready to ask questions. The key was letting them experience it themselves—people don't learn theoretically, they learn experientially. In many cases, a coach's role is to step out of the way and say, "Okay, go ahead and let's see what happens." If it doesn't work out, coaches can extend grace but also ask open-ended questions: "What could you have done differently?" Real-life consequences often prove the most effective teachers.

What further training would be helpful?

As people continue to progress, they may realize they have new areas they need to develop, which may lead to new agenda items in coaching relationships or particular areas on which they need to work.

I once worked with a man named Doug. His first agenda was time management. He was working at a church, working a secular job, and trying to balance his family life. As we worked together, Doug made progress and we celebrated that progress. When I asked him what further training would be helpful, he asked for help with financial management. He was having trouble with debt and overspending. We worked together to structure a budget, and within a year Doug was in a much better financial position. I've found that when you ask people where they need additional help or training, they usually know.

What's next in our coaching relationship?

One area that needs regular review is the coaching relationship itself. It's good to periodically think through where you are and what changes need to be made to make the relationship more productive. In some cases, you'll want to renew a commitment to working together; in other cases, the time is right for bringing closure.

Resist the temptation to assume that things are going fine unless you hear otherwise.

Resist the temptation to assume that things are going fine unless you hear otherwise. Rare is the person who will volunteer feedback to his coach, especially negative feedback. Coaches will need to initiate the process by having the courage to ask the hard questions.

Since a review of the coaching relationship won't arise naturally in most cases, having a built-in plan for evaluation from the beginning usually makes the most sense. Ideally, coaches will have monthly or quarterly evaluation forms designed to assess the relationship. These can be completed by hand or via email. Below are some sample questions. As holds true in the rest of coaching, open-ended questions will yield the most fruit.

- What would you like me to do more or less, or stop doing all together?
- What have you accomplished this month that you would not have done if you were not partnering with a coach?
- How do you feel about what you have and have not accomplished this month?
- What are some things I could do differently?
- What could I provide that would help you even more in achieving your goals?
- Do you feel I am pushing you enough, too much, or not enough?
- Where have I missed the mark this month?

Conclusion

We all need time to stop and catch our breath once in a while. Without time set aside for reviewing, we can find ourselves moving frantically from one project to the next without considering the value of our activities. By taking the time to evaluate our progress, we can gain a sense of perspective. Solid reviewing looks both to the past and to the future, for learning from our past—both the successes and the failures—gives us renewed strength and vision for the road ahead.

Your turn

How is the review stage both backward looking and forward looking? Give examples from your own life or ministry.

Field Work: Spend fifteen minutes reviewing your accomplishments over the past three months. Either write about them on your own or pair up with someone else to discuss them. Try to come up with at least ten accomplishments. They can be as big as running a marathon or as small as making your bed for the first time in weeks.

CHAPTER 7

Guidelines for powerful coaching relationships

Introduction

Steve was in training to become a Natural Church Development coach. He wanted to work with congregations to help them improve their overall health by administering the NCD survey, identifying the areas of church life most in need of change, then guiding them through the growth process. Steve was just beginning to work with some congregations and he wasn't sure how to structure his coaching relationships. Just saying, "Let me know how I can help you," didn't seem specific enough. The pastors wanted to know exactly what he was going to be doing and what they could expect. Steve wasn't sure what to tell them. He felt as if he were learning to swim.

Slowly, Steve learned how to set expectations at the beginning. How long will we work together? How often will we meet? In many cases he gave those he was working with choices, but just having a structure in place put them more at ease. They were able to establish goals and line up their action plans with the big picture in mind. Steve found that when people knew how much time they had with him and when, the process became vastly more productive.

So how do you put together a successful coaching relationship? What can you do to set it up for success? Although there will be different options and variables for different contexts, it's best to have certain pieces in place. This chapter covers the nuts and bolts of the coaching relationship, surveying a few key areas that merit discussion at the outset of that relationship. The recommendations made are based on years of experience. Yet far from being rigidly prescriptive, the material in this chapter is designed to prompt your thinking—issues to consider as you establish and support a coaching relationship.

Establishing clear expectations

Providing a clear structure and expectations for the coaching process from the beginning is essential for establishing and maintaining trust. In order to forge ahead, make changes, and reach an optimal level of effectiveness, people need to start from a safe place. Knowing what to expect and understanding the rules and the process of coaching play a big role in making the relationship safe.

How many friendships and dating relationships have broken up over unclear expectations? "You were supposed to ... " "You didn't ... " "Why did you ... ?" Clarifying and agreeing upon expectations up front goes a long way toward maintaining a healthy coaching relationship. Be sure to discuss assumptions about being on time, appointment cancellations, and commitment to address agreed-upon issues.

Three men formed an accountability group, a form of peer coaching. At the beginning, they agreed that it would be a group to keep them accountable for areas of temptation and weakness in their lives. However, they never expressly sat down to flesh out what that would look like. They all assumed they knew what that meant.

Over the course of the next few months, one man repeatedly expressed frustration: "I thought we were going to get specific about our behaviors and ask one another a series of questions each week." Another man disagreed: "No, it was supposed to be less structured than that. I figured we'd each have a turn to talk about what was going on in our lives while the others listened and provided support." The third man admitted, "Now that I think back on it, I'm not really sure what I expected." Within six months, the group disbanded. Differing expectations left everyone feeling disappointed.

Regularly scheduled meetings

If you are involved in a coaching relationship, it works best to have regularly scheduled meetings. The "call me when you need me" approach is rarely effective. People aren't sure when they need you, so they don't call and the coaching relationship slowly fades away. Meeting once or twice a month is a feasible option—less often than once a month can decrease effectiveness and every week can lead to burnout. In certain cases you may want to get together more frequently if you're coaching a person who is working on an intense project or issue, but weekly meetings shouldn't be the norm. At least one week a month should remain free to let people's thoughts settle and begin to percolate. The key is finding a pattern that will be effective, yet not overwhelming.

A thirty to forty-five minute session can usually accomplish whatever needs to be done. An hour should be the maximum length of a meeting—any time beyond that only wears people out. Whatever length of time you choose, be clear about when the session will end. Setting clear expectations demonstrates a respect for the other person's time. She knows how long she has to accomplish what she set out to do and she knows the session won't drag on indefinitely or interfere with her other activities. If coaching meetings are allowed to run indefinitely, people often keep talking until they run out of energy rather than ending on a high note.

A beginning and an ending

Like individual sessions, the coaching relationship itself should have an agreed upon beginning and ending point. Although beginnings are usually self-evident, endings are commonly overlooked. People often assume they'll just know when they're done. Yet not having a destination in mind changes the dynamic of the relationship itself. Momentum and motivation decrease. Without the structure an end date provides, people lack a place to move toward and can feel like they're just rehashing the same material over and over again. They begin wondering, "When

> **Although beginnings are usually self-evident, endings are commonly overlooked.**

do I ever get to the finish line and say I've completed the race?" The ending date may not be totally final, but it's a good practice to specify a certain length of time. At that point, the relationship can be reevaluated and a decision can be made about whether the relationship needs to be continued.

The optimal length of time for a coaching relationship is usually between three and twelve months. Joan planned to start a new outreach ministry at her church and wanted to get some coaching. She asked Sherilyn if she could do it for just a month. She had some travel plans coming up that would interfere with a longer commitment. Sherilyn declined, citing the importance of having a coaching relationship for at least three months. She explained that no change can become permanent in a much shorter period of time. The cycle of change involves initial progress, running into some roadblocks, then coming back up the other side and seeing that all the effort is making a difference—only then will changes become part of the fabric of someone's life.

Joan decided to wait on the coaching until after her trip and then committed to a longer process. After three months, she told Sherilyn, "I see now why you wouldn't let me do this for just a month. I would never have gotten to the place I am now if we had only met once or twice."

Just as there are minimums, there also ought to be maximums. Coaching is not designed to continue indefinitely, for the goal of coaching is gearing others toward independence. Once they've accomplished their initial goals, people can move forward in their lives using the skills they've learned. They may receive additional coaching in other areas of their lives or ministries. They may begin coaching others. Yet whatever course is chosen, coaching should never become a dependent relationship in which people need the coach in order to accomplish their goals. If that dynamic evolves, the coaching relationship was not healthy or successful. One year is generally enough time for people to learn new skills, internalize the changes, then tackle additional goals on their own.

Accountability

Accountability is one of the essential underpinnings of the coaching relationship—it's what gets things done. One easy way to ensure consistency is by using an accountability form at each session. When people write down the goals they want to accomplish by the next session, it's there in black and white for both them and their coach to see. In writing down goals and action steps, they become more definitive. Sometimes just knowing that next time they get together with their coach they'll review the form is enough to spur people to action.

Terry was a denominational leader. One of his goals was to write a vision letter that would be sent out to all of the pastors in his region. After putting it off for two months, Terry finally wrote the letter. On the accountability form at his next coaching session, he wrote, "Vision letter complete only because I didn't want to come to one more meeting without it finished." Regardless of whether an official form is used or not, having some type of structure in place helps people accomplish their goals more consistently.

Confidentiality

Since coaching requires that people be vulnerable enough to share their challenges and shortcomings, coaches often find themselves in positions of trust. Honoring that trust requires that information shared in confidence be kept in confidence. In order to work effectively on areas needing change, we need a safe environment. That means we know that what we share stays within the confines of the coaching relationship. No one wants to acknowledge an area of struggle, only to find out that other people suddenly seem to know about it.

A good rule of thumb is: if in doubt, don't say it. Of course, if a coach becomes aware that someone is a danger to himself or others, the rules of confidentiality no longer apply. In those cases, whatever steps are necessary should be taken to see that the person receives help.

The specifics of confidentiality should be clarified at the beginning of the coaching relationship. Eileen was talking with a man her husband was coaching when he began making references to issues he was dealing with, assuming that she knew about them. She had to stop him and explain that her husband never shared information from coaching relationships with her. After that experience, Eileen's husband wrote out his confidentiality policy and began making sure those he coached were aware of it.

Depending on the situation, it may even be a good idea not to divulge the identity of those you are coaching. In some cases, it won't make much difference—such as when an experienced worship coordinator is coaching a new worship coordinator. Yet in other cases, more personal issues may be easily conjectured. Keith, a man who had a history of multiple addictions, had been in recovery for ten years. When he began coaching others in his church, he kept their names confidential out of concern that assumptions would be made about the nature of the coaching relationships.

Safeguarding confidentiality also reduces the likelihood of facts being distorted. A missionary named Jeremy was home on furlough and got involved in a coaching group. Through that experience, he realized that many of the roadblocks he'd been running into were cross-cultural issues. Over the course of a few months, Jeremy realized he was not gifted cross-culturally. Shortly afterwards, he resigned from the mission agency and decided to serve at a homeless shelter in downtown Chicago, where he'd grown up. As Jeremy was talking with Bill, the director of the homeless shelter, Bill asked him, "Can you tell me more about why you left the mission field? I've heard some conflicting reports." It turns out that a man in Jeremy's coaching group told a friend who was on staff at the shelter, who passed along to Bill that Jeremy had been having cross-cultural problems with some of the women on the mission field. Breaking confidentiality is no different than gossip and can do just as much damage to a person's ministry, career, family, and reputation.

Setting goals

One of the most common mistakes new coaches make is not having the people they are coaching develop an agenda for the relationship. Out of a desire to avoid pressure, they approach the coaching relationship with an attitude of "So what should we talk about today?" Yet if both parties know ahead of time that three specific issues need to be addressed, coaching meetings can be much more fruitful.

At the beginning of the relationship, coaches can ask questions that will give them more insight into the other person's goals: "What three things would you like to accomplish in the next thirty to ninety days?" "What are three things that if you accomplished, you'd feel so delighted you were walking on air?" Compare their answers with any previously stated goals. As mentioned earlier, people often put forth the goals they think they should have instead of those they truly want. This is often the problem behind those action steps that are carried over from month to month and never taken—they represent goals that aren't truly owned.

> **Coaching is most effective when specific, measurable goals are set.**

No amount of coaching, structure, or accountability can make people do something they don't really want to do—something that isn't consistent with who they are or with what God has called them to do.

Coaching is most effective when specific, measurable goals are set. A generalized goal like "becoming the best leader I can be"—while an important starting point—will not be as helpful in the short-term as more specific goals such as reading a particular book, brainstorming on a topic, or reevaluating a schedule.

Setting boundaries

A relationship that is not defined is not safe. We need to know the rules and expectations the relationship is operating within so we can relax and focus on our goals. Can I call my coach outside of regular coaching appointments? Would I be bothering her? What about email? What are the boundaries of the relationship? Are we friends or is it purely professional?

The answers to these questions will differ depending on the circumstances and on the individuals involved, but questions will be asked—either explicitly or implicitly. Boundaries need to be clarified: when we meet, where, for how long, and what we do during those meetings. Clear parameters that are agreed upon ahead of time also help prevent any problems with the opposite sex. When people know in advance, "This is the only amount of time we're spending and this is all we're doing," they are more free to focus on the task at hand.

When Sherilyn coaches in a professional capacity, she has the boundaries of her coaching relationships clarified on paper: the expected number of sessions per month, unlimited email support, and brief, ten minute phone calls for very focused conversations if problems arise. One day Sharon called her in tears. Sharon was an actress, but due to lack of current work, she had decided to teach for a year at a local high school. The decision had been a hard one, and she was now doubting herself. She wondered if maybe she shouldn't be doing this after all. Together, Sharon and Sherilyn went over the reasons she had decided to teach temporarily, focusing on her values, her priorities, and her long-term strategy. Through their conversation, Sharon began to feel reassured that she was not settling or selling out her dreams. After reviewing the big picture, she recognized that even though things were hard right now, this was still the best decision for her in the long run.

Defining roles

As you work to set realistic expectations for a coaching relationship, keep in mind the three rules of coaching:

1. The person being coached does the work.

2. The person being coached does the work.

3. The person being coached does the work.

If people don't do the work themselves, they won't learn. It's like learning your multiplication tables. If you always have someone there to supply the answer, you'll never learn them for yourself.

Letting people know about the three rules of coaching up front can help avoid false expectations of "help." Sometimes people enter into a coaching relationship thinking that their coach will ensure the accomplishment of their goals. Although coaching does provide helpful structure and accountability, it still boils down to the person being coached doing the work. There's no magic wand.

The coaching agreement

How often to meet, how long to meet, accountability, confidentiality, goals, boundaries, expectations . . . it can begin to feel overwhelming. That's why it's a good idea to put it all in one place at the beginning of the coaching relationship—in a coaching agreement. A coaching agreement, sometimes called a coaching covenant, can be likened to a syllabus received at the beginning of a class. A syllabus defines the parameters of the class, outlining major areas such as subject to be studied, textbooks, evaluation methods, and any other expectations. It basically covers the rules by which the class will be run. By looking at a syllabus, most students can get a pretty good idea of whether this is the class they wanted. If not, there's still time to drop it.

Likewise in a coaching relationship, it's best to outline the parameters and expectations clearly at the beginning so the people being coached know what they're getting into. If this isn't what they wanted, it's much better to find out now than two or three months down the road. Once an agreement is made, both people understand the general expectations and know they're on the same page.

Ideally, a coaching agreement will be tailored to the situation at hand. Although overlap will certainly exist in different types of coaching relationships, coaching church planters will look different from life-management coaching or career coaching. Any agreement will need to be adapted to the specific area of coaching and to the personalities and preferences of the individuals involved. Take some time to look over books and websites on coaching to get an idea of what's out there. We've also included a sample coaching agreement in the appendix. Once you've reviewed some options, put together your own agreement—one that will make sense in your coaching context.

Using online coaching tools

Many coaches have found it beneficial to add an online element to their coaching relationships. It's not designed to be a substitute for face-to-face or phone coaching, but a tool to significantly improve the quality and focus of the time you have together. Personally, I've found that using an online process to prepare for sessions in advance and to follow through afterward has easily doubled my coaching effectiveness. Online coaching provides built-in structure, allowing for easy tracking of goals, prayer requests, action steps, and agenda items. Although such structure can certainly be built into traditional coaching relationships, many people—even those who meet in person regularly—find it easiest to prepare, organize, and track progress in one place: online.

When people use online coaching tools to prepare in advance, they know they're dealing with the issues that are the most significant to those they're coaching. They're also able to follow up on those issues more easily. One man described the added accountability online coaching brought him: "Once I write something down in that coaching log, I either have to make an excuse or celebrate getting it accomplished. If it's down in front of me on a list of tasks that need to be completed, I know I'll be meeting with someone soon who will hold me accountable for my level of completion."

Completing coaching logs online also makes for easy continuity of record keeping. In looking back over the summary, people can see the long-term process. Viewing the whole history of what's been accomplished gives people a big picture perspective—an especially important benefit for times of difficulty or discouragement.

Many coaches have found that online coaching saves preparation time, making meetings more efficient. The specific agenda can be set before each meeting, allowing everyone to come prepared and on the same page. One coach who had been briefed for a meeting ahead of time arrived having already reviewed a key document, commented on it, formed some questions, and brought along a few potential resources. In essence, she was able to dialogue with the team she was coaching with all the preliminaries out of the way—they'd already been covered in the coaching summary. Online coaching can vastly increase the effectiveness of regular meetings by managing appointments, recording and monitoring progress, and streamlining information sharing within the relationship.

I use online coaching in all my coaching relationships. I find that its real power is in helping people prepare in advance, which greatly enhances both face to face meetings and follow up. To find out more about online coaching tools, visit *www.coachnet.org*. Far from being impersonal, online coaching tools help make the personal time that much better.

Dealing with conflict

Unfortunately, not everything can be dealt with ahead of time in the coaching contract. If only life were that clean and easy. Coaching relationships are made up of people and people will—if they are honest—have conflicts. Some form of conflict is inevitable—it's just a matter of time.

Once a coaching relationship has been established, dealing with conflict when it arises is one of the most essential ways of supporting and maintaining the relationship. To remain effective and focused, the coaching relationship must be kept free of encumbrances. Whatever the nature of the conflict, it will need to be addressed promptly.

A coach named Sam shares one of his experiences with conflict:

"A question from a couple of group leaders I coach hit me the day before I was going on vacation. Bill and Rachel had been having trouble with children during their small group meetings for quite a while. How to cope with the several toddlers whose parents attended the group was a complex, ongoing issue that we had examined from several different angles in the past. So Bill called just before my vacation and left me a message wanting to know if the church had any money budgeted for small groups that could be used for child care.

"After checking with the trustees and some staff members, I was faced with a decision. I could either take the time to invest in explaining the situation or I could just go for the quick fix. I went for the quick fix. I wrote an email saying that no, no money was available. I added a couple of lines of poorly worded explanation about what kinds of things the church should pay for and what was individual responsibility, then I sent it off.

"They were understandably upset about the way I'd handled it—and they were right. Basically, I communicated an issue of policy about groups via email when I should have sat down with them and explained the reasoning behind the decision. The big issue wasn't around the policy decision itself, but around the way I chose to communicate it. Email has no tone. There are certain things you can communicate using email, but there are others you can't. The temptation with technology is to try to solve problems quickly using email and I did that. I went after the quick fix and it didn't work. That was an important lesson for me to learn as a coach.

"After Bill responded to my email, I realized I'd been wrong and I needed to hear how my actions had affected them. I went back and sat down with them to really listen and validate their concerns. Bill was upset and expressed his feelings, but Rachel said, 'Yeah, it seemed a little curt, but I didn't have a real problem with it.' At that point I had to draw her out by saying, 'I'm serious here. I really want to know how that impacted you.' As I began to invite Rachel and Bill into that process, I discovered that taking the time to listen well can help rebuild trust.

Frequently asked questions

Is it ever appropriate for males to coach females and vice versa?

We believe the answer to this question depends largely on what type of issues you're working through in the coaching relationship. One ministry leader coaching another through the launch of a new ministry would be appropriate across gender lines in most cases, while delving into more personal issues may not be. Remember in any case that coaching is not counseling.

In I Timothy 5:1-2, Paul writes, "Treat younger men as brothers, older women as mothers, and younger women as sisters, with absolute purity." The guideline for any cross-gender relationship is absolute purity. Therefore, don't hesitate to set any personal boundaries you feel appropriate. Some denominations or groups may have rules on these matters, so by all means follow your convictions and live within the guidelines of your organization.

Above all, use common sense. Don't put yourself in positions that would potentially be a problem. Maintain a sense of professionalism *and be sure you are relating to others with absolute purity. Whatever it takes for you to do that, that's what you need to do.*

What should I do if the person I'm coaching isn't fulfilling his responsibilities?

It's happened to all of us—we haven't gotten our work done, we've been out of the office, we've forgotten appointments. We haven't necessarily been irresponsible—we've just had a wild ride the last month or so. Everybody has a season where life goes crazy. When someone you're coaching starts dropping balls, a number of possibilities exist. Ask yourself whether the problem is purely circumstantial. Has there been a recent family medical crisis or some other emergency? Or is this more of a patterned way of living? If the issue is circumstantial, a break from coaching may be in order. After all, coaching isn't supposed to increase stress, it's supposed to help relieve it.

The best advice we have for discerning why people are not fulfilling their responsibilities is to talk honestly with them about it. Don't skirt the issue. Try to engage them in open discussion: "Here's what I've observed. You've come up with things you want to do, but they don't seem to get done. What's up?" Let them know it's okay— it's not like they're getting a bad grade. You just want to find a better way to help them. You may want to ask them some of the following questions: Is what we're doing working for you? What's working? What's not? Do you really want to do this? Is the goal you've set something you really desire? What are you committed to? What are you willing to do to get there? Is what I'm doing helpful? How can I help you more effectively? Then have them set an agenda and action steps based on their own responses.

Remember that coaches don't succeed or fail on the basis of whether people follow through or not. I used to take it personally when people didn't follow through. Those you are coaching are the ones setting the agenda. They're in control, and they're the ones who chose to work with you. Revisit what they want. You may need to do that often even when it was laid out at the beginning. By letting those you are coaching control the agenda, you're freed up to be truly helpful. Their agenda frees you: because it's their agenda, they can do it or not—it's entirely up to them. Coaches can get overrun with "shoulds" too.

What should I do if I need to step down from the coaching relationship?

As coaches, we should have stated terms under which we work with people. A good coaching agreement specifies a length of time you're committed to the coaching relationship and builds periodic reviews into that time frame. Ideally a coach should wait for the scheduled reevaluation time to close the coaching relationship. However, under extreme circumstances, this may not always be possible. If at some point you need to end a coaching relationship, explain the reasons or circumstances, schedule a closure session, and be sure to provide a list of other coaches the person can contact if he wishes to continue working.

How should I respond if I discover the person I'm coaching has serious underlying issues of which I wasn't aware?

Sometimes during the course of coaching it becomes apparent that the person you're coaching needs to be seeing a counselor. If you run into that situation, know your limitations and don't hesitate to get the person connected with someone who can help. Certain cases are clear-cut matters for counseling: depression, eating disorders, mental illness, addictions, abuse, affairs. These types of problems require more help than you can give as a coach.

In other cases, deciding when a counseling referral is necessary is a more intuitive process. Marital issues that are negatively impacting a person's ministry can sometimes be resolved by simple strategies: committing to spending more time together and being held accountable to that commitment through coaching, for example. Yet other patterns continue getting in the way regardless of strategizing. When you as a coach find yourself thinking, That really needs to be fixed, recognize that counseling may be in order.

I once coached a planter who seemed to be continually overwhelmed. No amount of energy we put into time-management skills or delegation was helping. I finally asked what was going on and he explained that he had a deeply rooted sense of drivenness that had been in place since childhood.

"Do you think it would be helpful to get counseling?" I asked.

"Yeah, I think so," he responded.

"How would you like to be held accountable?"

He thought for a moment.

"Probably just by asking me if I followed through on keeping the appointment."

While counseling helped him work through some of the triggers and drivers of that compulsion to succeed, we were able to continue working on the practical end of things related to his church plant.

Sometimes it's helpful just having another person acknowledge that a particular issue is a problem.

Sherilyn finds that when serious problems surface during coaching, the coach can be most helpful just by making sure the person gets help sooner rather than later. She once worked with a woman who struggled with bulimia, and one of this woman's coaching goals became following through with getting help. Encouragement, follow-through, and accountability can play significant roles in the healing process.

Coaching is very behavioral. If a person can't change the problem by changing a behavior, recommend counseling. Does the problem go away or is it more deeply rooted? The goal of coaching is to work on a particular issue, but sometimes something bigger and deeper keeps short-circuiting it, undercutting it, and dismantling it. That's when referrals to counseling or a twelve-step group are appropriate. Coaches don't have to do it all and be able to handle anything—we're just here to come alongside.

Conclusion

Setting clear guidelines at the beginning of a coaching relationship is crucial. Take the time necessary, whether verbally or in writing, to lay out clear expectations for how the process is to be approached. When we know what to expect, we are freed to focus our attention and energy on the task at hand, setting things up for success at the outset. Providing some structure and clarity will greatly enhance the usefulness of the coaching relationship.

Most people come into a coaching relationship uncertain about what to expect. They look to the coach to set norms for the relationship. As a coach, don't be afraid to step in and spell out the expectations. Far from feeling boxed in, most people will appreciate the clarification. Of course, be open to dialoguing about what each of you would like the relationship to look like, but know in advance which areas are nonnegotiable for you. Having your own standards clearly in mind will help you know the degree of flexibility you can have with others.

Your turn

Field work: Establish a coaching relationship with someone. Consider the seven questions below and formulate a coaching agreement based on them.

- How often will we meet?

- Where will we meet?

- How long will each coaching meeting last?

- In what ways will we be in contact at other times and for what purpose? (e.g. through email, phone, **CoachNet's** online coaching tool)

- What commitments will we make? (e.g. confidentiality, follow-through)

- For what initial period do we want to have a coaching relationship? When will we evaluate our effectiveness?

- What do you want to focus on during the coaching relationship? What issues are you sensing the Holy Spirit prompting you to address?

Chapter 8

Where do I go from here?

Introduction

To quote one of our favorite coaching questions . . . what's next? Now that you've read about the five Rs of the coaching process—relate, reflect, refocus, resource, review—what can you do to begin growing as a coach? We offer two recommendations: keep it simple and get started.

The temptation to wait until you know what you're doing is strong. The problem is, we can't really know what we're doing until we've started doing it. A beginning therapist once complained to an experienced colleague, "Sometimes I feel like the people I'm working with are guinea pigs. I don't know if what I'm doing is helpful or not. I wish I already had ten years of practice under my belt so I'd know what to do."

His colleague responded, "No one starts out an expert. The only way to get to where you want to be is through experience—there are no shortcuts."

The same is true of coaches: no one starts out completely competent. In order to build skills and gain proficiency, we need to dive in and get some experience. Sometimes that'll

> **No one starts out completely competent.**

mean we make mistakes. That's okay—it's part of the learning process. Becoming a better coach means getting started and finding out where you need to grow. Once you pinpoint growth areas, remember that plenty of help and resources are out there. But for now, all you need to do is get started. The material in this book gives you everything you need to begin coaching, and the rest of this chapter outlines some suggested first steps.

Skill building activities

Wherever you are and whatever your current skill level may be, you can engage in these activities and gain increasing competence as a coach. We recommend that you start with the following:

Start acting like a coach

Act like a coach by practicing a coaching lifestyle. When your child asks you a question, engage in conversation instead of just giving a quick answer. When people involved in ministry come to you with a problem, take the time to draw them out instead of focusing on giving solutions. Ordinary daily life—provided you live it with your eyes and ears open—offers you countless opportunities to practice coaching skills.

I recently picked up a friend in my car to take him to church. He began telling me he had just been promoted to a supervisory role at work and was getting some negative responses from his former peers. Instead of offering sympathy or giving advice, I started asking him questions about his desires and his options. Giving that man a ride to church was an ordinary activity and we were having an ordinary conversation, yet I found I still had the opportunity to practice coaching skills. You don't need to be involved in a formal coaching relationship to engage people in the discovery process.

Some of you may be new to coaching; others may be experienced leaders. In either case, you may find you have some bad habits to overcome in order to become more effective coaches. Try some of the following everyday-life exercises: Force yourself to use only open-ended questions for a whole day—no yes/no questions allowed. Whenever you find yourself wanting to make statements or give advice, ask a question instead. Take note of people's body language. Compile a list of good questions and see how many ways you can use them in different situations. Practice reflective listening skills with a spouse or friend and take note of their response. When essential coaching skills are practiced creatively in everyday life, they can encourage the development of good, long-term habits.

Practice in triads

A few years ago I was consulting with a denomination that wanted to design a comprehensive coaching process. They'd already done a lot of coaching with their church planters, but until now had not applied it to the pastors of existing churches. As I dialogued with the pastors, I sensed their reluctance to form one-on-one coaching relationships with one another. They were concerned about pride and competition for the mentor/coach role. They viewed coaching as supervisory and didn't believe it could be experienced as a peer relationship.

That's when I introduced triads. Triads are excellent for peer-coaching relationships and can be one of the least intimidating options for those just getting started as coaches. By meeting together with two other beginning coaches, you can take risks and try out new ideas in a safe, nonthreatening environment. Triads are the perfect place to practice, develop, and hone your coaching skills, gaining the confidence necessary to take those skills into other areas of life.

Here's how triads work: three beginning coaches meet for an hour and a half once a month. Each member has already been trained in basic coaching skills—the group may even elect to read and work through this book together. Each person gets half an hour to talk about a real-life situation, while the other two act as coaches. No focus-shifting is allowed; it is not a free-form discussion, but a disciplined process within a structured timeframe. At half-hour increments, participants switch roles so each person has the opportunity to receive undivided attention and two opportunities to practice coaching. The coaches share the load so the pressure isn't all on one person, allowing for more peer-level relations and additional insight.

One group of pastors who formed a coaching triad found immediate and powerful results. Needs started being met as they experienced the power of a caring and supportive community. The pastors were amazed at what a rare gift it was to receive half an hour of focused attention and the opportunity to process without interruptions or someone saying, "Here's what happened to me . . . ." This brief exercise of only an hour and a half a month gave them each a taste of what coaching could be, along with a sense of excitement that they could pass this gift along to others.

Cultivate coaching in your relationships

Become more intentional about incorporating coaching into your existing relationships. Consider your coworkers, kids, spouse, parents, friends, and ministry-team members. Just about any relationship you have can benefit from the use of coaching skills. Remember: coaching isn't about setting yourself above others in order to teach them. It's about listening and asking good questions to draw them out. Identify those in your life who could benefit by your practice of coaching skills, and intentionally cultivate a coaching approach to those relationships.

In addition to your natural network of relationships, consider those people with whom you could develop a formal coaching relationship. At the beginning of this book, you were asked a question: "Who has made a difference in your life by coming alongside you as a coach?" Now we're asking a different question: "Who can you coach? Who can you come alongside and help as a brother or sister in Christ? Where will you make a difference?" Now is the time to pass on the blessings that have been given to you.

Who can you coach right now where you are? Consider the possibilities that are currently available. Could you coach new Christians? New leaders? To what groups or individuals do you feel most drawn? Remember that coaching includes all areas of life, not just ministry in the local church. The skills you're developing are applicable at all levels, in all relationships. When you have some ideas with whom you'd like to enter into a formal coaching relationship, take the initiative to meet with that person. Be intentional and set up an appointment. You can make a difference by starting wherever you are.

Get a coach

The best way to learn how to coach is to get a coach. As Sherilyn says: "One of the greatest things about having a coach myself was experiencing how all the things I knew on an intellectual level came together in real life. I'm glad I experienced the power of coaching in my own life because it makes me more sensitive to those I coach. I understand how they feel, and that helps me communicate more effectively. It was also a great opportunity to get sample resources, forms, structures, assessments, and tools from my coach mentor." Many resources are available that can help those new to the field make connections with coach mentors—seminars, coaching companies, networks, or online resources such as *www.coachnet.org*.

Advice for new coaches

I was once asked what advice I would give to help people get an effective start as coaches. I came up with six thoughts and I'd like to share them with you as well.

- Sometime within a few days of finishing this book, make an appointment with yourself for an hour and a half to sit down and process the material provided here. It's easy to forget if you wait longer than that. Set down in writing action steps, ideas that seem important to you, questions you have, brainstorming, and areas you need to study further.

- Set an appointment with yourself for two hours once a month to continue tracking the coaching process. Implementation is a step-by-step process requiring a long-term strategy.

- Consider forming a triad with other coaches. Meeting together once a month for an hour and a half should provide a structure that will keep you on track and provide accountability.

- Begin putting something in place to train others in your church in basic coaching skills. You don't need to cover all the material in this book, but offer something that will help others enter into this process.

- Go onto CoachNet's website (*www.coachnet.org*) and check out the coaching tools available.

- Begin with the end in mind. Consider the long-term impact of your ministry and your choices. When you look back at the end of your life, what legacy do you want to leave behind?

Coaching: a spiritual process

Developing coaches have a lot to learn: listening, asking questions, relating, reflecting, refocusing, resourcing, reviewing. Mastery of these skills will help us become more effective coaches. It's our duty to be as prepared as possible.

Yet be sure not to lose sight of one central fact: It's God who is ultimately at work. We can do all things only through him who gives us strength. God is the one who works through coaching relationships, causing growth and transformation. He is the one who speaks the words into our ears that will bring about deep, lasting change. He is the one who directs our steps, who closes some doors and opens others.

Coaching is God's territory, not ours. For all our skills, we are but tools in his hands, ready and available to be used.

God chooses to work through people—and his choices are often surprising. He doesn't always use the most well-trained, talented, together people. He uses those whose hearts are open to him. If no one fitting that description is available, he'll use donkeys or stones (Num. 22:28, Luke 19:40)—it doesn't matter. God will bring about what he wills.

He calls us to diligently prepare. He calls us to open ourselves to the unexpected, stepping out in faith when we feel like we're in over our heads. Paradoxically, both are true. For our God is a God of paradox. He is three-in-one, the Alpha and the Omega. He works in mysterious ways—and in not-so-mysterious ways. Our duty as coaches is to train hard, then run the race on his strength.

Seeing people through God's eyes

Coaching lets us see into the hearts of others. One of the sweetest rewards coaches receive is being allowed those fleeting glimpses into other people's lives. Sometimes, just briefly, we can see them as Jesus would see them. That's a powerful honor for coaches, and—if handled well—a gift to those who are being coached.

A successful and well-loved pastor, now retired after leading a large church for decades and planting several daughter churches, remembers a significant statement made early in his ministry. He was just out of seminary and discouraged about finding work when his coach told him, "You are important to me, to God, and to the church . . . and I believe that God can work through your life." That was a critical turning point for the pastor. That statement from his coach was the gift of knowing that someone believed in him.

God calls us to look past the surface, past charm and charisma, past current failings and flaws, to see the unique imprint of God's image on the lives of others. As coaches, we are called to see not just who people are now, but who they could become.

Erin bought a house. It was an old Victorian house and in need of some work. A week after she moved in, water began leaking from the ceiling. A month later the furnace stopped running. After having to make additional repairs to the pipes and the stairs, Erin began feeling worn out and discouraged.

Yet whenever she walked through the front door and saw the old fireplace, she felt hope. Spanning almost a whole wall, it was one of those grand, imposing old structures, made of hand-wrought iron and surrounded by brick. Although tarnished by years of neglect, Erin could see the promise in it. She scrubbed it for weeks, taking off layer after layer of black grime, until the metal gleamed and its former glory was restored.

Erin didn't make or design the fireplace; she just uncovered what was already there. She was able to look past the unappealing and the mundane to see the masterpiece that lay beneath. It's the same with coaches—we have the privilege to see and develop what God has already placed within people. Our vision and hard work serve only to reveal the possibilities that are already present.

"For I know the plans I have for you," declares the Lord, "plans to prosper you and not to harm you, plans to give you hope and a future" (Jer. 29:11). Prosper is a strong word—it connotes a sense of abundant and overflowing joy. God does not want to make us just acceptable enough to get by, serviceable and nothing more. He has lavish possibilities in store.

Your Turn

What thoughts or ideas stand out to you most as you finish this book?

_____

_____

What are the next steps God is calling you to take?

_____

_____

Field work: Make a definite plan to release the power of coaching in your life. Jot your thoughts down in the space below and write out your prayer of response to God.

"The purposes of a man's heart are deep waters, but a man of understanding draws them out." Proverbs 20:5

APPENDIX

Powerful Coaching Questions

RELATE

1. How are you doing?
2. Where are you now?
3. How can I be praying for you?
4. What do you want to address?
5. How can we work together?

REFLECT

1. What can we celebrate?
2. What's really important?
3. What obstacles are you facing?
4. Where do you want to go?
5. How committed are you?

REFOCUS

1. What do you want to accomplish?
2. What are possible ways to get there?
3. Which path will you choose?
4. What will you do (who, what, when, where, how)?
5. How will you measure your progress?

RESOURCE

1. What resources will you need to accomplish your goals (people, finances, knowledge, etc.)?

2. What resources do you already have?

3. What resources are missing?

4. Where will you find the resources you need?

5. What can I do to support you?

REVIEW

1. What's working?

2. What's not working?

3. What are you learning?

4. What needs to change?

5. What else needs to be done?

6. What further training would be helpful?

7. What's next in our coaching relationship?

Sample Coaching Agreement

Below is a sample coaching agreement between a lay coach and a new small group leader who would like help getting his group started. You can adapt this agreement to fit your context, goals, and preferred guidelines.

Agenda and goals

The focus of the coaching relationship is to help launch a new small group. Initial goals include the recruitment of apprentices, the recruitment of group members, the establishment of healthy group norms, and learning more effective ways of facilitating group discussions.

Meetings

We'll meet twice a month for the first two months as the group is being formed, then once a month after that. Meetings will take place on Thursdays over the lunch hour at a restaurant halfway between our offices and will last for forty-five minutes.

Additional contact

If questions arise, I am available via email and phone. Preparation for our meetings will be done online at www.coachnet.org at least two days prior to each scheduled meeting.

Commitments and expectations

1. Be on time for appointments.

2. Call if you need to cancel or reschedule.

3. Commit to addressing the agreed-upon issues and following through on assignments. All goals and assignments will be set down in writing via online coaching to avoid miscommunication and to ensure accountability.

4. Confidentiality will be maintained except where permission is expressly granted or where disclosures affect the ability to continue serving in a ministry capacity.

Length of coaching commitment

We'll begin coaching March 1 and work together for three months. At that point, we'll evaluate the effectiveness of the coaching relationship and the present situation and make a decision as to whether it would be beneficial to continue for another three-month period.

Additional Coaching Resources

Coaching 101 Handbook

The **Coaching 101 Handbook** is a resource designed to help leaders apply the practical principles introduced in **Coaching 101** and begin the journey of becoming a more effective coach.

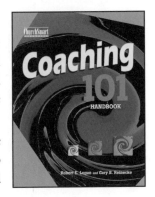

You will gain a deeper appreciation of the coaching process and "coming alongside" to help others as you understand the model outlined in these pages:

RELATE – establishing a coaching relationship and agenda

REFLECT – discover and explore key issues

REFOCUS – determine priorities and action steps

RESOURCE – provide support and encouragement

REVIEW – evaluate, celebrate and revise plans

The **Coaching 101 Handbook** is packed full of practical ways you can improve your skills in coaching those God has brought your way. Discover the power of coaching and the adventure God has in store for you and those you coach. Tomorrow will never be the same!

Retail: $10.00

Developing Coaching Excellence

Developing Coaching Excellence is a resource designed to motivate leaders to excel at coaching. The research-based coaching process, competencies and sound Biblical principles give a comprehensive framework for all your coaching relationships. Building off the coaching process found in the *Coaching 101 Handbook*, **Developing Coaching Excellence** will help you improve your overall

effectiveness as a coach so that you can achieve coaching excellence.

You will discover five assessment methods to determine your coaching effectiveness along with a step-by-step process to help you identify action steps in a Personal Development Plan.

You will be challenged to master nine coaching competencies that research has shown will help leaders clarify a personal or group mission so they can cooperate with God to advance the Kingdom and achieve their goals.

FOUNDATIONAL COMPETENCIES
Abiding in Christ
Self-assessing
Communicating

RELATIONAL COMPETENCIES
Establishing
Supporting
Concluding

STRATEGIC COMPETENCIES
Diagnosing
Planning
Monitoring

Discover the adventure God has in store for you, those you coach and those you train as coaches. It can make a difference …forever.

Retail: $75.00

Contact Information

Dr. Bob Logan
CoachNet International Ministries
Web: www.coachnet.org
E-mail: Logan@coachnet.org

Sherilyn Carlton, M.S.
Destination Coaching
E-mail: Carlton@destinationcoaching.com